'With her joyful approach and simple-to-follow recipes, Melissa has created the ultimate kitchen companion for families.'
Skye Gyngell, chef

'I have never met anyone who screams "real food" more than Melissa Hemsley.'
Sarah Wilson, author of *New York Times* bestselling *I Quit Sugar*

'Melissa's recipes are rooted in the wisdom and science that whole plants are the cornerstone of a healthy diet.'
Dr Federica Amati, PhD MPH RNutr, author and head nutritionist at ZOE

'A treasure trove of delectable and approachable recipes.'
Rachel Khoo, food writer and broadcaster

'A delightful guide to shifting the focus onto eating more plants, cooking more intuitively and fostering a more sustainable and wholesome approach to mealtimes.'
Dr Saliha Mahmood Ahmed, NHS gastroenterology doctor, author and *MasterChef* winner

'In a time when ultra-processed foods are all too common, *Real Healthy* stands out by bringing wholefood cooking back to life.'
Sarah Ann Macklin, ANtur, registered nutritionist, founder of Live Well Be Well podcast and the Be Well Collective

'Melissa's done the very difficult thing of hitting a great balance of encouraging healthiness without compromise on flavour and pleasure.'
Mark Diacono, author and food writer

'Whether it is time that you are pushed for, your kitchen confidence needs a boost, or you simply want to carry on eating good, enjoyable family food that cares for your health too, *Real Healthy* will give you everything you need.'
Dale Pinnock, nutritionist and chef on *Eat Shop Save*

'I talk a lot about adding "extras" into family meals to help up the veggies and also increase the nutrition of our family foods – this book offers plenty of extras with fresh and nutritious ingredients, but in really simple recipes with lots of store cupboard ingredients too.'
Charlotte Stirling-Reed, the baby and child nutritionist

'Melissa is one of the most trusted people around. This book is so simple and helps us to understand so clearly why we all must make changes.'
Gaby Roslin, broadcaster and author

Real Healthy

Unprocess your diet with easy,
everyday recipes

Melissa Hemsley

EBURY
PRESS

Contents

Foreword

by Rhiannon Lambert, registered nutritionist, bestselling author, podcast host and founder of Rhitrition

In a western world where cooking from scratch has taken a back seat in recent years, *Real Healthy* emerges as a beacon of light for everybody looking to live a happier, healthier life. Melissa is not giving bespoke nutrition information as she knows that one size does not fit all, rather she is providing the tools you need to re-evaluate your dietary choices, while offering practical solutions for embracing a more wholesome way of eating, without compromising on taste.

The prevalence of ultra-processed foods (UPFs) is concerning as they have taken over the traditional value of a home-cooked meal, making up a significant portion of our diets due to their convenience and palatability. The health consequences of excessive UPF consumption cannot be overstated, now potentially linked to a whole host of health ailments, such as obesity, cancer and other chronic diseases. In my Rhitrition clinic, I've witnessed the profound impact that dietary choices have on one's overall health and well-being, and how mental health in particular can be drastically affected by the foods we eat.

With an array of easy-to-follow recipes, accompanied by storecupboard suggestions and batch cooking tips, Melissa equips you with the tools you need to embark on a journey towards wellness that starts in the kitchen. In today's fast-paced society, nourishing ourselves adequately has become increasingly difficult, with limited time for meal preparation and grocery shopping, paired with soaring food costs and household expenses. The Big Batch, Lots of Veg Bolognese and Aubergine, Tomato and Butter Bean Traybake recipes are perfect examples of how cooking from scratch can be quick, simple and cost effective, yet benefit our health so much more than convenient on-the-go meals.

Beyond its culinary offerings, *Real Healthy* serves as a guidebook for embracing a new lifestyle rooted in whole foods and mindful eating. Melissa's thoughtful approach empowers you to make informed choices about your dietary habits, encouraging you to re-evaluate the proportion of UPFs versus whole foods on your plate. *Real Healthy* is more than just a cookbook; it is a guide to reclaiming our health, revitalising our relationship with food, and safeguarding the future of our planet. May this book serve as a guiding light for all those embarking on their journey towards real, lasting health.

Introduction

As the horrifying headlines have rolled in about ultra-processed foods (UPFs), I worried about what I could do to be part of the change. I wondered if there was a way I could write a hopeful, healthy, helpful antidote to all the scary statistics.

I'm lucky to have been brought up on meals mostly made from scratch. My mum worked full-time and it must have been a challenge to cook from scratch like she did, let alone the arguments about me eating what she prepared – as a child I didn't necessarily want to eat her healthy food! I know that, having learned so much from being in the food industry for 15 years, it's easier for me to eat healthy whole foods and not have to rely on UPFs. Having said that, I've become more determined than ever to help others get back to cooking basics; to remind them of the knowledge they already have – and to help them navigate the things they find tricky so they can make healthier choices. To share the simple pleasure that comes with turning a few basic ingredients into a wholesome, flavour-packed bowl of food that you will LOVE and feel nourished by – and will eat again, and again.

So welcome to *Real Healthy,* a book of easy, doable and delicious recipes that will slot into your everyday routine, and your whole family will enjoy. This is a cookbook full of whole food and veg-packed dishes based around minimally-processed ingredients.

What we eat every day should be simple, but for so many of us food has become complicated and difficult. We have limited time to cook, limited time to shop and busy lives to juggle, not to mention rapidly rising food and home costs. The world has become about convenience and immediacy, shortcuts which allow us to continue living our lives at an ever-increasing rate, without stopping to think about whether the choices we're making best serve us.

In the food world, these convenient shortcuts usually take the form of ultra-processed foods, a term which very generally means foods that are highly altered, highly palatable and that contain ingredients you wouldn't add when cooking at home (more on exactly how to recognise these later). UPFs have become a hot topic of late, thanks to the fact that the UK population eat more than any other country in Europe, with

a massive 57% of our energy intake coming from UPFs[1] (this number is even higher in under 14s).

Like many people, I've found it impossible to ignore the conversation about the negative effects UPFs are having on our overall health and general wellbeing. For example, research has shown that they've been linked to many serious illnesses, yet still the average person in the UK gets over half of their calories from UPFs.[2] In addition, if a plate is filled with UPFs this can lead to less room for those (plant) foods we are encouraged to eat more of – like fruits, vegetables, whole grains, beans, lentils, herbs, spices, nuts and seeds.

These recipes are about amping up the whole foods and vegetables on our plates and dialling down the ultra-processed foods.

The statistics around UPFs can sound alarming. PLUS they're not that straightforward to identify, not always clearly labelled and, as a result, some of us are eating more than we think. But rather than dwell on frightening figures or the impacts of these foods, this book is about practical, simple and delicious ways to reduce our reliance on them. I hope to make real healthy home-cooking as convenient as possible, as time is the most precious ingredient of all!

Simply put, the easiest way of cutting back on UPFs in your diet is to cook food from scratch using simple and whole ingredients. Now, this is easy to say, but can be difficult to put into practice when you've got an endless to-do list, and/or limited time to spend cooking and shopping. My experience is that most of us are looking for a helping hand when it comes to meal planning because we're busy and time-poor. For some meals we can't help but rely on the convenience of takeaways, ready meals and the deliberately designed appeal of familiar packaged and super-processed food.

In *Real Healthy*, I've taken care to think about the areas that so often trip us up, those times when the easiest option is often the UPF-heavy, veg-light, shop-bought one. Breakfasts in a rush or missed completely, an often expensive lunch at your desk, bought from a high-street chain, a snack, energy drink or sweet treat to get you over that 4pm slump. I'm going to help you plan so that at the end of the day you can put a tasty, satisfying, veg-packed meal on the table – one that the whole family will appreciate. In this book, you'll find healthy, nutritious alternatives that you can prep ahead and use to help readdress the ratio of less processed food to ultra-processed food that ends up on your plate.

I am not a doctor, nutritionist, or expert in UPFs and the effect they have on our health. I'm also not suggesting that completely cutting out UPFs is necessary or even possible. (Nothing will ever make me give up ketchup and I'm not here to say you can't eat crisps.) This is not a book to demonise the way anyone chooses to eat, and it is not a diet book – you won't find calorie counting or macro breakdowns here.

I simply hope that the recipes and tips in this book will help you if you're looking for ways to cut back on UPFs, or to disrupt your reliance on convenient takeaways, low-veg-count ready meals and those can't-stop-eating-keep-you-wanting-more snacks.

For example, instead of a pre-packaged breakfast cereal, why not try making a big batch of **Cherry Almond 'Bakewell' Granola** (page 32) to start your day? If you find yourself dashing to the nearest lunch food chain every time you're in the office, I've got a whole chapter of recipes you can pack up at home and take with you like **Big Veg Noodle Salad with Lime, Ginger and Peanut Dressing** (page 50), or **White Chicken Chilli** (page 62). If you have very little time to cook in the evenings, and UPF ready meals have become a useful crutch, there are chapters on 30-minute meals, one-pot dinners and traybakes, which I hope will take a lot of the stress out of weeknight cooking. Think **DIY Ciabatta Pizzas** (page 78), **One-pot Lasagne** (page 142), **Ginger Spring Onion Salmon** (page 113), or **Rainbow Rice with Omelette Ribbons** (page 85).

As well as 90 flavour-packed and wholesome recipes, I've also included inspiration for some different ways to enjoy them (see pages 20–1) to help you make the most of cooking up a big batch. As well as this, you'll find my **Top 10 UPF tips** on page 14, alongside suggested short lists of go-to ingredients that you might like to keep in stock in the freezer, fridge and cupboards to make your meal planning and weeknight cooking easier than ever.

This book is for anyone who loves food – whether you love to regularly cook or not – and for everyone who loves hearty and delicious meals, which are quick to pull together and hit the spot every time.

What are ultra-processed foods?

There's no simple definition of ultra-processed foods but, generally, you could say that they: a) contain more than five ingredients; b) come pre-packaged and c) contain preservatives, emulsifiers and sweeteners. They tend to have a longer shelf-life than fresh foods and are designed to be highly palatable, so that you want more and more and more of them. A (slightly oversimplified) way of thinking of them is: if a food contains ingredients you wouldn't find in your home kitchen, it's most likely ultra-processed.

As I said, it's not necessarily straightforward. Not all ultra-processed foods are 'bad' or as 'bad' as each other. For example, additives are important in some foods. Baked beans and sliced wholemeal bread would be classed as UPFs but arguably have more nutritional value than a bag of flavoured crisps or a long-life cake. There are also foods that might fall into both the 'processed' and 'ultra-processed' categories, depending on the brand you buy (things like ready-made sauces, yoghurt or peanut butter, for example). I've outlined below how you can start to identify UPFs, but it's worth remembering that even the experts disagree on some of these points. (Although this may change as the conversations around UPFs get louder and more mainstream.)

What's the difference between processed and ultra-processed foods?

Humans have been processing food for centuries. Pretty much every bite of produce we eat has been processed in some way (washed, cleaned, packaged, frozen, ground, churned, pasteurised). In our home kitchens, and in cafés and restaurants, we are processing our food when we slice, roast, fry, steam and boil it, too. So, it's important to distinguish between 'processed' food and 'ultra-processed' food.

As of 2023, the UK government has not given formal dietary recommendations for UPFs.[3]

Currently most people refer to the Brazilian NOVA classification system, which groups foods into four general categories:

1.   **unprocessed or minimally processed food** (e.g. fruits, vegetables, eggs, fish, meat, grains, milk, legumes)

2.   **processsed culinary ingredients** (e.g. butter, salt, sugar, plant oils)

3.   **processed food** (e.g. fresh bread, tinned pulses, fermented or cured foods, cheese, beer and wine)

4.   **ultra-processed food** (e.g. most breakfast cereals, confectionery, ice cream, mass-produced bread, pre-packaged meals).

Although it's complex, it can be a useful guide to sort foods in your head.

Some UPFs are obvious and easy to spot, for example sweets, chocolate cereals and fizzy energy drinks. Others are less obvious, for example stock cubes and bottled sauces. Some UPFs are marketed to seem healthier than they are, e.g. protein bars or packaged smoothies with 'health halos'. More work needs to be done on national guidance and clearer labelling, but with a little bit of digging and reading of packaging, you can usually make a pretty good assessment of what you're buying.

For more information on resources, see page 223, and I'd especially recommend reading *Unprocessed* by Kimberley Wilson, *Ultra-Processed People* by Chris van Tulleken, *Food for Life* by Tim Spector and Rhiannon Lambert's *The Science of Nutrition*.

Why should we care about UPFs?

It bears repeating that this book is not telling you to cut out UPFs or dictating how to eat. What you eat is up to you! But I know from meeting many of you at book events or chatting on social media that lots of you are also hoping to readdress what percentage of your day-to-day foods are dominated by UPFs. In an average working week, it's all too easy to end up grabbing UPF-heavy foods for breakfast, lunch and snacks, maybe even dinner too.

I eat and enjoy UPFs (I don't know anyone who doesn't!). I personally love a tub of mint choc chip ice cream, a biscuit with my cup of tea, and a sharing bag of chilli lime tortilla chips with a gin and tonic. In my cupboards and fridge doors, you'll spot tomato ketchup, a jar of a shortcut sauce, a favourite ready-made curry paste and a chocolate bar (or two or three)! All of these, which would be classed as UPFs, are delicious, comforting, familiar and part of many of our food habits, loves and rituals.

However, as of 2022, household purchases of vegetables dropped by 14%[4], and recent studies identify ultra-processed foods as the primary cause of early deaths, globally.[5]

For the next generation of teens, not only is 67% of their daily energy intake made up of UPFs but research shows the knock-on effect is that with UPFs making up a great proportion of their plate, there's less space for healthy whole foods, which may disrupt their future palates and food habits.[6]

We need a healthier, more honest food environment for everyone.

We shouldn't feel wholly responsible for this. It's our government, policy makers and the big food industry players who have the power to curb the rapid spread of UPFs and reorganise our food system for the better for everyone in society. But right now, we can do something about it personally. I started cooking as a private chef when I was 23 years old and I've been sharing healthy recipes for a decade, but I'm now even more passionate about being part of a healthier, more honest food environment for everyone. And especially since the publication of the latest global research, including a recent *British Medical Journal* study, which states that 'Greater exposure to ultra-processed food was associated with a higher risk of adverse health outcomes, especially cardiometabolic, common mental disorder, and mortality outcomes'.[7]

A final note on the privilege of choice

We can't talk about UPFs without acknowledging how they fit into our daily lives. The alternative to a UPF-heavy diet – choosing whole, unprocessed ingredients and cooking from scratch – is not possible for everyone. It's important to recognise that not everyone has the luxury of choice or the opportunity to feed their families certain foods, or even has access to an oven, or the time for a weekly shop or to eat at the table with their loved ones. There are many people living with chronic illnesses or disabilities, for whom ready-meals and pre-packaged foods are essential to their survival. Cooking snacks, breakfasts and sweet treats from scratch takes time and a certain degree of planning ahead, all luxuries that are not available to everyone. Not to mention that the cost of living crisis and rising food prices mean that shopping for fresh, local produce is not an option that fits into many households' budgets.

I've tried my best to ensure that the ingredients in these recipes are as accessible as possible and have kept ingredients lists shorter than previous books. To make your time in the kitchen count, I've thought about minimising hands-on cooking time and washing up, so you'll find let-the-oven-do-the-work traybakes, 30-minute meals, one-pot wonders and lots of recipes which create leftovers that roll over into lunch the next day.

For those of us who *do* have the privilege of choice, we can keep voting with our spending power in the shops and every time we eat out. The more we keep the conversation going about 'more whole foods, less ultra-processed foods' and readdress the balance, the more the large food companies will look to change up their products. Our government(s) need to prioritise addressing food policy. Let's band together and keep asking those in power for clearer labelling, more honest marketing, less junk food advertising for our kids, and an improvement in food product formulas too. We can do more than hope for better; we can keep showing up for ourselves and the next generations. If we ignore the rapid rise in UPFs or accept their ubiquity, we will move further and further away from real healthy food and all its technicolour flavour, benefits, pleasure, nourishment and joy!

Top 10 UPF tips

Here are my top tips for those of you looking to cut back on UPFs. From how to recognise them, to not stressing too much about how many you're eating, I hope this will help you if you're looking to reduce the percentage of UPFs in your diet.

1. **Don't pressure yourself.** A good place to start is to try not to stress – this isn't a new diet or regime and no one is telling you what rules to follow. If anything, the only guide I'd offer is 'make more of the foods that make you feel good'. Enjoy.

2. **Turn it over and read the label.** Different brands of products may mean that you can buy a UPF or minimally processed version of the same ingredient (e.g. peanut butter). There are no hard and fast rules and product formulations change – so get to know your labels. There are also apps to help you identify products both in store and online. Once you get into the swing of it, you'll find it easier to look out for products that you DO want to take home with you.

3. **Have whole foods on hand.** Build up a foundation of storecupboard staples and stock up on some fridge and freezer essentials (see pages 16 and 19 for ideas) so you've always got the building blocks of a quick meal on hand for those evenings you get caught short and don't have time to dash to the shops. For example, a tin of chickpeas and your favourite spice mix in the cupboard, greens in the freezer and tomato purée and yoghurt in the fridge.

4. **Containers.** Stock up on reusable jars (old honey or jam jars work well) to use for breakfasts on the go or to store layered up lunch salads. You might also find it useful to invest in a flask for hot drinks like the Sunshine Tea on page 205, and for taking hot food on the go like the White Chicken Chilli on page 62. I have a few leakproof containers for freezing or safe fridge storage. Always try to label with the date, you always think you'll remember and then you don't!

5. **Team up.** Join forces with a colleague or friend to share food here and there. It's always easier to create a new habit or try new things with someone else involved. One of you could make snacks for the 4pm

slumps and the other could make a batch of soup to enjoy as a working lunch, then the next week you swap around.

6. Meal plan. I'm not suggesting you need to suddenly sit down every Sunday and write a meal plan for the week. But for the times you find yourself leaning hard on UPFs (e.g. working lunches or breakfasts) some meal planning at the beginning of the week can help you avoid the same pitfalls each time. Letting your kids choose a dinner recipe each week might help encourage them to try new ingredients or get more interested in cooking.

7. Food prep… both for foods you love to eat and foods you'd like to eat more of! Think of your favourite foods, and the ones you make again and again. For example, do you enjoy lots of roast vegetables, tomato sauce or broccoli? Maybe make a big batch of them once a week to save you time. And are there foods that you'd like to eat more of? Perhaps salad and lentils. Try prepping some of these ahead and making a jar of salad dressing so that you're more likely to enjoy them.

8. Batch cook. By this I don't mean eating the same leftovers four nights in a row (unless you want to!). I grew up with a mother who championed 'cook once, eat twice' so I often find myself making a bigger batch of something so that I can freeze half for a rainy day (check out the Big Batch, Lots of Veg Bolognese on page 168). Or you can pick dinner recipes that will give you rollover leftovers for lunch the next day (like the Throw-it-all-in Lentils on page 144).

9. Swaps. It's so easy to get stuck in a shopping rut, so why not pick something in each weekly shop to switch it up? One week it could be trying a different sort of salad leaf – chicory instead of baby gem lettuce, for example – then the next it could be trying a different grain like pearl barley instead of rice. Not only does this keep us from getting bored of the same foods but means we are gaining so much more diversity in what we eat.

10. Mindful eating. I know this term makes some people's eyes roll but we have a lot to learn from our bodies. I find it helpful to observe how I feel after eating certain foods, how they affect my mood, energy levels etc. If I have an energy slump, get a headache, or find myself feeling jittery or have a bit of brain fog, I try to avoid eating these foods during the week when I'm juggling work, parenting and already feeling stressed. If I notice certain foods keep me happy and satisfied until the next meal, I'm inspired to eat more of them.

UPF-free favourites

Our shopping baskets are often full of convenience foods – bottles of salad dressings, tubs of hummus, packets of crisps, chocolate hazelnut spread, pastries, biscuits and sweets, wraps, cereals, flavoured or low-fat yoghurts, jams, breads, instant pot noodles, packet sauces, stock cubes and spice pastes. These products have their place and not all are always UPFs, but the recipes in this book show you how to make your own to decrease the ingredients you don't need and increase those you might want more of – veggies, whole grains, pulses, herbs, spices and healthy fats. There's lots of pleasure to be had from making your own versions at home and I don't know about you but when they're a pleasure to make AND quick AND effortless, then it's a win-win-win!

Here's a list of some of my favourite ingredients to keep in stock in your freezer, storecupboard and fridge, so you'll always have ingredients on hand to be able to throw together the recipes in this book.

5 freezer faves

1. **Spinach**

2. **Peas and edamame**

3. **Mixed berries**

4. **Sweetcorn**

5. **Quality meat and fish or chicken broth** (or in fridge)

UPF-free favourites

10 countertop and fridge faves

1. **Eggs**

2. **Dairy** – butter, cheese and yoghurt

3. **Flavour boosters** – miso paste, kimchi, harissa, pesto, chilli sauce (make your own, see pages 200–1)

4. **Leafy greens** – kale, chard, rocket, salad, fresh herbs

5. **Root veg** – potatoes, carrots, squash

6. **Courgettes, mushrooms and bell peppers**

7. **Cruciferous veg** – broccoli, cauliflower, cabbage

8. **Citrus** – lemons, limes, oranges

9. **Ginger, garlic and onions**

10. **Fruits** – bananas, apples, pears

10 storecupboard essentials
(go for different varieties where possible)

1. **Chickpeas, beans, lentils** (tinned or jarred)

2. **Nuts and seeds**

3. **Sea salt, spices and dried herbs**

4. **Maple syrup/honey/dried fruit**

5. **Rice/quinoa/mixed grains/oats**

6. **Tomatoes** (tinned or jarred)

7. **Noodles and pasta**

8. **Olive oil** for frying, **extra virgin olive oil** for dressings and drizzling, and **vinegar**

9. **Coconut milk and tamari/soy sauce**

10. **Tinned oily fish,** including sardines, mackerel, anchovies

3 ways with...

Some of the most asked questions I get are: 'What's the best way to meal prep in a easy way?' 'How can I batch cook and not get bored eating the same thing?' And, 'Give me ideas for quick meals on busy nights, please!' So I've taken four of my favourite recipes and given you three different and delicious ways to enjoy them by changing up how you serve them. Hopefully this will inspire you for your own future meal planning.

Red lentil and tomato super sauce (page 160)

1.   Use as a simple, supercharged **sauce for spaghetti**. Or add capers, jarred roasted peppers and a splash of red wine vinegar to make a version of the Peperonata Pasta on page 86.

2.   Blitz with a splash of stock (or even just water) to **make soup**. Delicious with fried halloumi on top, or with grilled cheese on toast for dipping.

3.   Use as the base for a **shakshuka** (add a pinch of smoked paprika for a little heat), perhaps with some spinach thrown in at the end for extra veg.

Curried root veg soup with crispy chickpeas (page 54)

1.   Scatter **with sticky spicy seeds** (see page 208) **or crispy beans** (see page 82 for how to do this but use whatever beans you have in the cupboard).

2.   Top with **fried halloumi, a little lemon zest and juice**.

3.   Leave it unblended and stir through cooked grains (pearl barley or rice would be delicious here), to turn this into a **hearty stew**.

Big batch, lots of veg bolognese (page 168)

1. Use as a base for a **shepherd's pie**. See page 150 – this version is extra simple as it's topped with sliced potatoes that become lovely and crispy in the oven, saving you the faff (and washing up!) of making mashed potato.

2. Add kidney beans (or a tin of mixed beans) and **serve with baked potatoes**, soured cream, grated cheese and pickled jalapeños. This is great if you're feeding a crowd because everyone can stuff and top their own potatoes!

3. **Toss with your favourite pasta** – I love rigatoni because the sauce gets into the tunnels. Or turn into a lasagne – see One-pot Lasagne on page 142.

Herb and mushroom breakfast slices (page 29)

1. Have a big slice **with a salad or slaw** for dinner.

2. Enjoy **in a sandwich** for a packed lunch.

3. Serve up **in small bites on a sharing board** with dips and olives and extra cheese if you're having people round or for an on-the-sofa snack plate.

Breakfast and brunch

I don't know about you but a delicious nutritious breakfast helps set me up for the day and has a positive knock-on effect far beyond the morning as it encourages me to make more considered choices for the rest of the day. But, for many of us, just grabbing something in a rush on the way to work is an achievement. It can be enough to simply get ourselves and in some cases our families ready on time, let alone make sure we've all had something nutritious to eat. This is why UPF options like breakfast cereals, long-life pastries or just simply skipping breakfast and going straight to coffee have become such commonly held habits.

In this chapter, I wanted to give you lots of options for things that can be prepped ahead so that you've got a less processed option ready to be thrown into a container as you grab your bag on the way out the door.

If you love oats in the morning, check out the **Banana Oat Breakfast Bake** on page 26, **Apple Ginger Bircher** on page 34 and **Berry Almond Butter Overnight Oats** on page 37. And for those of you who like to start your day with a bowl of cereal, the Bakewell Tart vibe of the **Cherry Almond Granola** on page 32 is going to make it your new obsession.

If, like me, you're into a savoury breakfast, the **Herb and Mushroom Breakfast Slices** on page 29 will be a particular favourite as they set you up with veggies and protein for the day, as do the **Frittata Muffins** on page 30, which you can customise so that in one tray of muffins you've got different flavours so you don't get bored having them several times in a week.

There are some other great breakfast options scattered throughout the book as well. Look out for the **One for Now, One for Later Banana Bread** (I freeze one loaf, page 174) and **Flatbreads** (page 202) which I love smothered with **Fetamole** (page 66) and topped with a fried egg.

For more breakfast inspiration, see **How to Build a Smoothie** on pages 40–1.

Banana oat breakfast bake

Feeds 4
Takes 45 minutes (only 10 minutes
hands-on time)

Butter or coconut oil, for greasing
2 ripe bananas
180g rolled oats
400ml milk or plant-based
   alternative
4 tbsp maple syrup or honey
2 tsp ground cinnamon
3 tbsp nut butter or tahini (stirred
   well in the jar first)
Small pinch of sea salt
Yoghurt, to serve (plant-based if
   you prefer)

FOR TOPPING
1 big handful of pumpkin seeds
   or chopped nuts
1 ripe banana, thinly sliced
   into coins

This is delicious warm from the oven but also great the next day or the day after, either cold (it goes lovely and squidgy from all the bananas) or reheated. Serve with a dollop of yoghurt for extra creaminess. Use plant-based milk and yoghurt if you prefer.

————————

Preheat the oven to fan 180°C/gas mark 6 and grease a large baking dish (I use one that's 29 x 23cm) with a little butter or coconut oil.

In a large bowl, mash the bananas. Add all the other ingredients, mix well, then transfer into the prepared dish. Scatter over the pumpkin seeds or chopped nuts and top with the banana coins. Bake for 35–45 minutes until set and golden at the edges.

Leave to cool slightly for about 10 minutes, then serve with yoghurt.

Herb and mushroom breakfast slices

Feeds 4–6
Takes 45 minutes

4 tbsp olive oil
250g mushrooms, roughly chopped
8 eggs
1 bunch of spring onions,
  finely sliced
2 large handfuls of soft fresh herbs,
  such as chives, flat-leaf parsley,
  basil or baby spinach, chopped
1 heaped tbsp Dijon mustard
2 handfuls of grated hard cheese or
  crumbled soft cheese
4 tbsp flour (I like using chickpea
  flour for extra breakfast protein)
Sea salt and black pepper

Tastes like a quiche and just as good the next day, so it's ideal for a few days of breakfast on the go. It's also flexible on the cheese and herbs: I love chives and parsley but basil, tarragon or dill would also be delicious. Try grated Cheddar, crumbled feta, whatever needs using up.

———————

Preheat the oven to fan 180°C/gas mark 6. Line a medium baking dish (I use a 20cm square one) with baking parchment.

Set a large frying pan over a medium-high heat, add 2 tablespoons of the olive oil and, once hot, add the mushrooms, plus a pinch of salt and pepper. Fry for 8–10 minutes until all their liquid has drawn out and evaporated off and the mushrooms are browned.

As the mushrooms fry, in a large bowl, whisk the eggs with a pinch of salt and pepper, then add the remaining 2 tablespoons of olive oil, the spring onions, herbs, mustard and cheese. Then add the fried mushrooms. Mix well so that everything is incorporated and evenly distributed. Lightly stir in the flour, then transfer to the lined dish. Bake for 25 minutes until set and golden. Enjoy straight away or keep in the fridge for up to 3 days.

Frittata muffins

Makes 12 muffins
Takes 25 minutes

Olive oil, for greasing
8 eggs
250g cherry tomatoes, quartered
1 handful of fresh chives, finely
  chopped
50g Cheddar, finely grated
100g cottage cheese (optional)
1 large handful of baby spinach,
  chopped
Sea salt and black pepper

As with 'proper' large frittatas, these are a great way to use up any odds and ends of veg, herbs and/or cheese in your fridge. Make them your own. Cottage cheese is a super popular ingredient these days – it's back from the 80s – so if you have half a pot that needs eating, it makes a great addition to the muffin mixture.

———————

Preheat the oven to fan 180°C/gas mark 6 and grease a 12-hole muffin tray with olive oil.

In a large mixing bowl, whisk the eggs and season with salt and pepper. Stir through the cherry tomatoes, most of the chives (hold back some for topping) and the Cheddar, plus the cottage cheese, if using.

Put the spinach in the bottom of the greased muffin holes. Spoon in the batter and sprinkle with the reserved chives and some black pepper. Bake for 12–15 minutes until set. Enjoy straight away or keep in the fridge for up to 3 days.

Smoothies

Each smoothie feeds 2–4 and
Takes 10 minutes

Whether you want a fast breakfast on the go or a mid-afternoon snack, smoothies are a great way to get some fruit along with some ingredients that pack in the protein and offer good fats. Adding a little black pepper helps you to get maximum health benefits from the turmeric. Try swapping some of the liquid for kefir or probiotic yoghurt. *(See How to Build a Smoothie, pages 40–1.)*

Pineapple, turmeric, ginger and lime smoothie

200g frozen pineapple (also delish
  made with mango)
1 small frozen banana
Thumb of fresh ginger
½ tsp ground turmeric
1 tbsp nut or seed butter
A little black pepper
Juice 1 lime
400ml water, or 200ml water and
  200ml coconut milk (for piña
  colada vibes!)

Put all the ingredients in a blender and blitz until smooth and creamy. Serve straight away or pour into a bottle to enjoy on the go.

Summer berry and almond butter smoothie

200g frozen berries
1 small frozen banana
½ tsp ground cinnamon
400ml your fave milk, or 200ml milk
  and 200ml water
1 heaped tbsp almond butter
1 tbsp chia seeds

The chia seeds help make the smoothie more substantial and keep you feeling fuller for longer, but you can leave them out if you don't have them. I love to go for a mixture of frozen berries, such as strawberries and raspberries, for plant diversity.

Put all the ingredients in a blender and blitz until smooth and creamy. Serve straight away, or pour into a bottle to enjoy on the go.

Cherry almond 'Bakewell' granola

Makes 2 large jars
Takes 45 minutes

250g rolled oats
125g pumpkin seeds
100g whole almonds
100ml olive oil
80ml maple syrup
1 tbsp ground cinnamon
⅛ tsp sea salt
100g dried sour cherries

The combination of almonds and cherries gives this granola major Bakewell tart vibes! If you're as much of a granola household as we are, you may want to make double, from our experience this goes in a flash!

———————

Preheat the oven to fan 180°C/gas mark 6. Line a large baking tray with baking parchment.

Weigh all the ingredients, except the sour cherries into a large mixing bowl. (The sour cherries don't get baked because they would burn in the oven, you'll stir them through the granola later.) Mix well so that all the dry ingredients are evenly coated with the wet ingredients. Spread out on the lined baking tray and bake for 30–40 minutes, stirring every 10 minutes for the first 20 minutes, then every 5 minutes for the second 10–20 minutes.

Allow to cool completely on the baking tray, then stir through the sour cherries. Store in airtight containers for up to 3 weeks.

Breakfast and brunch

Apple ginger Bircher

Feeds 4
Takes 10 minutes, plus
overnight chilling

200g rolled oats
2 tbsp chia seeds
2 handfuls of toasted nuts or seeds,
  roughly chopped, plus extra
  to serve
2 apples, cored and coarsely
  grated
1 handful of raisins or other dried
  fruit
Thumb of fresh ginger, finely grated
½ tsp ground turmeric
500ml milk of your choice
Honey or maple syrup, to taste

TO SERVE
200g yoghurt or your fave coconut
  yoghurt
4 handfuls of berries (fresh or
  frozen) or sliced banana and/or
  apple, sliced into matchsticks

Bircher needn't ever be the boring virtuous choice. You could have a different Bircher flavour every morning of the week, but here's my favourite combination with apple, turmeric and fresh ginger for that lovely kick. Your Bircher can be stored and served in reused jam jars for grabbing and going. Make a big batch once a week – it will take you 10 minutes. If you'd like more diversity in your diet, try a mix of oats with quinoa flakes or oats with buckwheat flakes. Change up the apple for pear and if you love berries, when they're not in season, frozen berries can be stirred through as they'll defrost in the mix overnight.

———————

The night before you want to eat your Bircher, mix all the ingredients in a large bowl, adding honey or maple syrup to taste depending on how sweet you like things, bearing in mind that the fruit and milk add natural sweetness. Cover and pop in the fridge overnight.

To serve, spoon the Bircher into bowls and top with yoghurt, extra fruit and chopped nuts or seeds. You could layer into jam jars for a breakfast on the go!

Breakfast and brunch

Berry almond butter
overnight oats

Feeds 4
Takes 15 minutes, plus
overnight chilling

200g oats
4 tbsp almond butter
2 tsp ground cinnamon
500ml milk (dairy or plant-based)
Tiny pinch of salt
2–3 tbsp honey or maple syrup,
  to taste
1 large handful of chopped
  almonds

FOR THE BERRY COMPOTE
300g mixed berries (frozen or fresh)
Juice of ½ lemon
1–2 tbsp maple syrup, to taste
1½–2 tbsp chia seeds

Use your favourite nuts, plus frozen or fresh berries or cherries. If you want to get fancy, you can make a 'parfait' by layering a few spoonfuls of the oats layer, then the compote and then the oats, etc.

———————

For the berry compote, put the berries, lemon juice and maple syrup (to taste) in a pan and simmer for 5–10 minutes until the berries have burst and softened. Remove from the heat and stir in the chia seeds, using the full 2 tablespoons if you prefer a thicker compote. Leave to cool, then cover and refrigerate overnight, alongside the overnight oats (below).

In a large bowl, mix the oats, almond butter, cinnamon, milk, salt and honey or maple syrup to taste. Stir to combine, divide between 4 jars or airtight containers and refrigerate overnight.

In the morning (or whenever you're ready), top the oats with the compote and chopped almonds.

Green beans on toast

Feeds 2 (makes extra
green sauce)
Takes 10 minutes

200g spinach
1 garlic clove
1 large handful of basil leaves
3 tbsp extra virgin olive oil,
  plus extra for drizzling
50g feta
Pinch of chilli flakes, plus extra
  (optional) to serve
1 x 400g tin of butter or cannellini
  beans, drained and rinsed
2 slices of sourdough bread
Sea salt and black pepper

Be generous with your handful of basil leaves, as it gives these beans such a lovely flavour and brings some summer sunshine vibes to the kitchen even on grey days. Top with extra feta if you like, or a fried egg. This makes extra sauce that you can stir through pasta for a quick meal or freeze for another day.

———————

Put the spinach and whole (peeled) garlic clove in a pan of salted boiling water and cook for 2 minutes until the spinach is wilted and dark green. Drain and squeeze out the excess water.

Transfer to a blender with the basil, olive oil, feta, chilli flakes and a few twists of black pepper. Blitz until completely smooth and taste for seasoning, adding a little salt if needed and more chilli flakes, if you like.

Put the beans in a pan (use the same one that you blanched the spinach in to save on washing up) and gently warm through over a medium-low heat. Once warm, add about half the green sauce (save the rest for pasta or freeze) and cook for a minute or two until everything is hot. Don't cook the sauce for too long, otherwise it will lose its lovely colour.

Meanwhile, get your bread in the toaster.

Spoon the green beans over the toast. Drizzle with a little more olive oil, and an extra pinch of chilli flakes, if you like.

Breakfast and brunch

HOW
TO
BUILD
A...
smoothie

Warming spices

Ground turmeric and black pepper, a pinch or two of ground cinnamon or a little fresh or ground ginger.

Something fruity

Frozen berries and cherries or tropical fruits, frozen or fresh banana and/or anything leftover from the fruit bowl, such as ½ apple or pear, or a squeeze of lemon, lime or orange juice.

Something green

Frozen spinach or a handful of fresh baby spinach, or herbs like fresh mint.

Ice

Add a handful of ice cubes before blending, unless your fruit is frozen.

Liquid

Water. Or try adding nut milk and coconut water, but I rarely do as it can get expensive. Another option is a little kefir or yoghurt, if you like.

Fat or protein

Nuts or nut butter or seeds or seed butter, such as chia seeds, flaxseeds and/or hemp seeds. You can also try ½ ripe avocado or 2 teaspoons of coconut oil.

Working
lunches

This is one of my favourite chapters because lunch during the working week seems to be a really tricky point for a lot of us. When we're having a busy day, it's all too easy to run to the nearest lunch food chain or end up grazing because we don't have anything better on hand. Even when working from home, it's hard to make time to step away from our laptops and make ourselves something delicious and wholesome to power us through the afternoon.

I'm often asked for packed lunch friendly ideas so these recipes have all been designed to be easy to pack-up-and-go. So, with a little prep the night before (maybe as you're tidying up dinner), you have something nutritious ready and waiting for you the next day.

It might be worth investing in some glass or stainless-steel lunchboxes, which should last you for years. You can get great ones with dividers so you can add some snacks as well (check out the Snacks chapter, see pages 197–217, for ideas). If you're packing up a salad like the **Green Goddess Salad** (page 58) or **Potato and Egg Salad with Purple Sprouting Broccoli** (page 49), you may want to put your dressing in a separate pot or jar to avoid soggy leaves come lunchtime. Grain, noodle, lentil and bean-based lunches like the **Herby Lentil Salad** (page 56) and the **Big Veg Noodle Salad** (page 50) can usually stand up to being dressed a few hours before, just make sure your container has a good seal so you don't get any bag leaks.

For hot foods like the **White Chicken Chilli** on page 62 and the **Curried Root Veg Soup with Crispy Chickpeas** on page 54, I recommend stainless-steel, insulated flasks. I'm still using one our family has had for 30 years, so they're well worth the investment!

See also **How to Build a Sandwich** (pages 68–9), **How to Build a Salad** (pages 70–1) and **How to Build a Lunchbox** (pages 72–3) and for more tips and ideas for quick and satisfying working lunches.

Sweet potato, chickpea and avocado salad with tahini dressing

Feeds 2
Takes 35 minutes

2 sweet potatoes, cut into
  bite-sized chunks
1 x 400g tin of chickpeas, drained,
  rinsed and patted dry with a clean
  tea towel
1 tbsp smoked paprika
1 tbsp za'atar or dried oregano,
  plus extra to serve
4 tbsp olive oil
2 large handfuls of salad leaves,
  rocket or spinach
1 avocado, cut into chunks
Sea salt and black pepper

FOR THE DRESSING
2 tbsp tahini
1 garlic clove, finely chopped
  or grated
3 tbsp extra virgin olive oil
Juice of 1 lemon

Chickpeas and tahini go perfectly together (hello hummus!) but here the chickpeas are roasted and then drizzled with a tahini dressing. This salad is ideal for a working lunch but it's so delicious that it's special enough for dinner too. Look out for purple sweet potatoes, which are fast gaining popularity in UK shops.

———————

Preheat the oven to fan 220°C/gas mark 9. In your largest roasting tray, toss the sweet potatoes and chickpeas with the paprika, za'atar or oregano and olive oil, then season with salt and pepper. Roast for 20–25 minutes until the sweet potatoes are soft and beginning to caramelise and the chickpeas are crisp.

Meanwhile, make the dressing by mixing all the ingredients together in a small bowl, then add 2–3 tablespoons of water to loosen it. Season to taste.

Pile the salad leaves, rocket or spinach onto plates, top with the roasted sweet potatoes and chickpeas and the avocado. Drizzle with the dressing and sprinkle over some extra za'atar.

Potato and egg salad
with purple sprouting broccoli

Feeds 2
Takes 30 minutes

250g new potatoes, halved or
  quartered if large
200g purple sprouting broccoli
4 eggs
1 handful of fresh parsley, tarragon
  or dill leaves
Sea salt and black pepper

FOR THE DRESSING
Zest and juice of 1 lemon
4 tbsp extra virgin olive oil
1 heaped tsp Dijon mustard
3 spring onions or fresh chives,
  very finely chopped

Any potatoes work well here but I love new potatoes in the spring and early summer months. Swap the purple sprouting broccoli for regular broccoli, or even asparagus when it's in season. I also love adding tuna, tinned sardines or smoked mackerel to this salad for that Niçoise feel.

———————

Put the potatoes in a large pan of salted water. Bring to the boil and cook for 10 minutes. Meanwhile, prep the broccoli by slicing any particularly large florets in half and chopping the ends of the stems. Add the broccoli to the potato pan to cook for 3 further minutes until the potatoes are tender and the broccoli is just tender. Lift the potatoes and broccoli out of the water, pat dry with a clean tea towel and set aside.

Keep the water on a strong simmer, then gently lower in the eggs and set a timer for 8 minutes.

For the dressing, mix all the ingredients (except a small handful of spring onions or chives for serving) in a bowl and season to taste. Toss with the potatoes, broccoli and herbs.

Once the egg timer has gone off, lift the eggs out of the water, run under cold water, then peel. Roughly chop the eggs, season with salt and pepper, then scatter on top of the salad and finish with the reserved spring onions or chives.

Big veg noodle salad with lime, ginger and peanut dressing

Feeds 2
Takes 15 minutes

2 nests of noodles
2 tsp toasted sesame oil
2 big handfuls of raw peanuts
1 large carrot, cut into ribbons
  with a peeler or cut into thin strips
  with a knife
¼ sweetheart cabbage, very thinly
  sliced
1 small apple or pear, cored and
  cut into matchsticks
½ small cucumber, diced

FOR THE DRESSING
2 tbsp smooth or crunchy
  peanut butter
2 big limes: zest of 1 and juice
  of both
2 tbsp tamari or soy sauce
Thumb of fresh ginger, finely
  grated
Pinch of chilli flakes
2 tsp maple syrup
Sea salt and black pepper

Even in the colder months, I think a big noodle salad is always a great thing to have up our sleeves. In the depths of winter, in and amongst all the cheesy bakes and big soups and stews, I crave fresh, zingy, crunchy salads like this. Use any noodles you like, even spaghetti would work if that's what you've got. I love buckwheat (soba) noodles. Swap the peanuts and peanut butter for cashews or almonds if you prefer. Do the lime trick to release more juice by rolling the limes on the kitchen counter before you slice them in half.

———————

For the dressing, whisk all the ingredients in a small bowl or shake in a jam jar. Taste for seasoning.

Cook the noodles according to the packet instructions, then drain and rinse immediately with cold water. Toss the noodles with the sesame oil and set aside.

Toast the peanuts in a dry frying pan over a medium heat for 3–5 minutes, shaking the pan every so often, until golden.

In a large bowl, toss together the noodles, carrot, cabbage, apple or pear and roughly half the dressing. Slowly add more splashes of dressing if you like, tossing as you go, until everything is nicely coated. Top with the cucumber and peanuts.

Butter beans and roasted peppers with chimichurri

Feeds 2
Takes 10 minutes

½ x 660g jar of butter beans or
  1 x 400g tin, drained and rinsed
150g roasted peppers from a jar,
  thinly sliced
½ cucumber, sliced (deseeded if
  you prefer)
1 avocado, sliced

FOR THE CHIMICHURRI
3 tbsp red wine vinegar
5 tbsp extra virgin olive oil
1 garlic clove, finely chopped
1 red chilli, finely chopped, or pinch
  of chilli flakes
1 large bunch of fresh parsley,
  finely chopped
Sea salt and black pepper

I definitely believe that beans make things better. Not only do they add heartiness to dishes but their mild flavour means they take on dressings and sauces so beautifully that they can also be the star of the show. I love a green sauce – it feels like every country has its own version of a herby green sauce (pesto, pistou, salsa verde, British mint sauce anyone?) Chimichurri is a very delicious green sauce that originates from Argentina and Uruguay. If you're packing this up for a working lunch, drizzle the avocado with a little vinegar or lemon juice to prevent it from turning brown.

———————

Make the chimichurri. In a large bowl, whisk the vinegar, olive oil and garlic together. Stir in the chilli and parsley and season to taste.

Add the butter beans, peppers and cucumber to the chimichurri. Toss and season to taste. Serve with the sliced avocado.

Curried root veg soup with crispy chickpeas

Feeds 4–5
Takes 40 minutes

800g mix of root veg (see intro)
4 tbsp coconut oil, ghee or olive oil
1 tbsp medium curry powder
1 large onion, roughly chopped
2 fat garlic cloves, roughly chopped
Thumb of fresh ginger, finely
  chopped
1.5 litres vegetable stock or broth
Sea salt and black pepper

FOR THE CRISPY CHICKPEAS
1 x 400g tin of chickpeas
3 tbsp coconut oil, ghee or olive oil
1 tbsp medium curry powder

TO SERVE
Greek or coconut yoghurt
Fresh coriander or chopped chives
Chilli flakes (optional)

The crispy fried chickpeas on top of this soup are always a hit. I love this with a medley of root veg – use whatever you've got. I make this a lot with carrots and sweet potatoes all year round, then pumpkin and butternut squash in autumn, and parsnips in the deepest, coldest winter months when we all need warming up.

———————

Preheat the oven to fan 220°C/gas mark 9 and chop the root vegetables into 4cm chunks (I don't peel the veg). Toss with 2 tablespoons of the oil, the curry powder and a pinch of salt. Spread them out as much as possible on a large tray and roast for 30 minutes until tender and caramelised.

Meanwhile, in a large pan, fry the onion, garlic, ginger and a pinch of salt very gently in the remaining 2 tablespoons of oil, stirring from time to time, until soft and golden, about 15 minutes.

Add the roasted vegetables and stock or broth to the onion mixture. Turn up the heat and bring to a simmer. Cook for about 10 minutes to allow the flavours to come together.

While that's simmering, drain and rinse the chickpeas. Pat them very dry in a clean tea towel so that when the chickpeas hit the oil they don't spit and can get as crispy as possible. Heat the oil in a large frying pan over a medium-low heat and, once shimmering, add the chickpeas and a good pinch of salt, being careful to stand back in case of spitting.

Fry for 6 minutes, stirring every so often, until crisp and golden. Add the curry powder and fry for another 2 minutes, stirring well to coat.

After the soup has had its 10 minutes of simmering, use a stick blender or food processor to blitz the soup, in batches, until smooth. Taste for seasoning before ladling into deep bowls and topping with the crispy chickpeas, yoghurt, fresh herbs, and chilli flakes, if you like.

Herby lentil salad
with hot-smoked salmon

Feeds 2
Takes 10 minutes

1½ tbsp your fave spice blend
  (I used a mixture of 2 tsp ground
  cumin, 2 tsp ground coriander
  and 1 tsp smoked paprika)
Zest and juice of 1 large lemon
4 tbsp extra virgin olive oil
1 handful of nuts, roughly chopped
1 x 400g tin of lentils, drained
  and rinsed
1 handful of fresh mint leaves,
  roughly chopped
1 handful of fresh coriander,
  including stems, roughly chopped
200g green grapes or cherry
  tomatoes, halved
2 hot-smoked salmon fillets
Sea salt and black pepper

A very speedy lunchbox salad that you could make for dinner and roll over leftovers into lunch if you like. It's barely got any cooking involved, just a quick toast of the spices to make the ingredients sing and then a quick toast of the nuts (any that you've got in the cupboard) to make their texture and flavour even better. Cook fresh fish if you like, but in a rush, I grab some hot-smoked salmon, mackerel or trout, always looking out for the responsibly sourced varieties. Puy lentils and green lentils are my favourite cooked tinned lentils.

————————

Toast the spices in a dry frying pan over a medium heat for a minute or so until fragrant, then tip into a small bowl along with the lemon zest and juice, olive oil and a generous pinch of salt and pepper (the lentils need to be seasoned generously). Whisk to combine.

Add the nuts to the pan, return to a medium heat and fry for a few minutes until golden.

Put the lentils, herbs, grapes or tomatoes and toasted nuts in a serving dish, drizzle over the dressing and toss. Serve with hot-smoked salmon, either flaked in or left as whole fillets.

Fried courgette, quinoa and quick-pickled red onion salad

Feeds 2
Takes 30 minutes

1 red onion, finely sliced
4 tbsp apple cider, red or white
   wine vinegar
100g quinoa, rinsed very well
1 handful of chopped nuts or seeds
2 tbsp olive oil
400g courgettes, cut into 2.5cm
   chunks
1 handful of fresh herbs, such as
   parsley or coriander leaves
100g feta
Sea salt and black pepper

FOR THE DRESSING
2 tsp mustard (I used Dijon)
4 tbsp extra virgin olive oil
2 tbsp vinegar
Good pinch of dried herbs or spice
   mix, such as dried oregano
   or za'atar

I love how flexible this salad is. Swap quinoa for rice or mixed grains for extra variety. Feel free to change up the nuts or seeds (some of my faves are cashews and pumpkin). For the vinegar, choose from apple cider vinegar, red wine vinegar or white wine vinegar. In colder months, I like swapping the courgette for roasted squash or sweet potato. The quick-pickled red onions are so worth making – add them to salads and sandwiches.

Put the sliced red onion in a jam jar or bowl with the vinegar and a little pinch of salt. Stir and scrunch the onions, then set aside to quick pickle.

Put the quinoa in a medium pan with 200ml of water and a pinch of salt. Bring to the boil, then reduce to a simmer and cook, covered, for 12–15 minutes until the water is absorbed. Turn off the heat and leave to steam for 10 minutes.

Meanwhile, put the nuts or seeds in a large dry frying pan over a medium heat and toast for 3–5 minutes until golden. Tip into a bowl and set aside. Return the pan to a medium-high heat, add the olive oil and, once hot, add the courgettes. Fry for 3–4 minutes until golden on the underside, then turn and fry on the other side for another 2–3 minutes until golden and tender. Season with salt and pepper and remove from the heat.

For the dressing, whisk the ingredients together in a bowl and season to taste. Fluff up the quinoa with a fork, then add to a serving bowl with the courgettes, herbs and the dressing. Stir gently, then top with the feta, toasted nuts or seeds and the quick-pickled onions.

Green goddess salad

Feeds 2
Takes 15 minutes (excludes
time for making a baked potato
to serve!)

1 baby gem lettuce, leaves
   separated
½ fennel bulb, finely sliced
½ cucumber, roughly chopped
1 handful of toasted seeds
   like pumpkin

FOR THE DRESSING
3 tbsp capers
3 tbsp yoghurt or plant-based
   alternative
3 tbsp extra virgin olive oil
Zest and juice of 1 lemon
2 handfuls of soft fresh herbs,
   such as parsley, basil, mint,
   dill or coriander, roughly torn
4 anchovy fillets (optional)
Sea salt and black pepper

I like to serve this with a baked potato or baked sweet potato but it's also delicious alongside leftover roast chicken or poached fish. This also makes extra dressing to keep in the fridge for up to 3 days. It's very loosely an ode to green goddess dressing, which comes from the San Francisco-style sauce that makes the Californian salads taste so good.

———————

For the dressing, blitz all the ingredients together in a food processor until smooth. Season to taste with salt and pepper.

Put the lettuce, fennel and cucumber in a large bowl. Drizzle over half the dressing, toss, then add more dressing if you like. Taste a leaf or two for seasoning, adding more salt and pepper as needed. Scatter over the toasted seeds and serve.

Roasted cauliflower grain salad with almond dressing

Feeds 4
Takes 30 minutes

1 head of cauliflower, cut into
  florets, stem chopped into
  small pieces
1 large red onion, cut through the
  root into thin wedges
4 tbsp olive oil
1 tbsp curry powder (or 1 tsp
  ground turmeric, 1 tsp ground
  cumin and 1 tsp ground
  coriander)
250g pre-cooked grains (to make
  your own use 100g uncooked)
2 large handfuls of soft fresh herbs,
  such as coriander, parsley, mint
  and/or dill
Sea salt and black pepper

FOR THE ALMOND DRESSING
75g whole almonds
2 tbsp extra virgin olive oil
2 tbsp apple cider vinegar
1 tsp Dijon mustard

How to combat soggy packed lunches? Use a sturdy veg like cauliflower, roast it and then combine it with a dressing that is on the thicker side, almost more saucy than splashy, if that makes sense?! This one holds really well, even once dressed, so it's good for packing up to take to work or on a picnic. I've enjoyed this with quinoa, rice, buckwheat and those helpful mixed grain packets from the shops.

Preheat the oven to fan 220°C/gas mark 9. Toss the cauliflower and onion with the olive oil and curry powder, then season with salt and pepper. Spread out on a large roasting tray and roast for 20 minutes until golden brown and tender.

Meanwhile, toast the almonds for the dressing in a dry frying pan over a medium heat for 4–6 minutes until golden. Put half in a small blender with the olive oil, vinegar and mustard. Blitz until smooth, then add 3 tablespoons of water and blitz again, adding another 1–2 tablespoons of water to loosen if needed. Season to taste. Roughly chop the remaining almonds.

Toss the roasted veg with the grains, dressing and herbs. Top with the chopped almonds.

White chicken chilli

Feeds 4
Takes 1 hour 10 minutes

4 bone-in, skin-on chicken thighs
2 tbsp olive oil, plus extra if needed
2 onions, finely chopped
2 yellow peppers, diced
4 garlic cloves, finely sliced
2 tsp ground cumin
1 tsp dried oregano
¼ tsp cayenne pepper or chilli
  flakes, to taste
1.2 litres vegetable or chicken stock
2 x 400g tins of white beans,
  drained and rinsed
200g frozen sweetcorn
Juice of 1 lime, plus a little zest
  if you like
Sea salt and black pepper

OPTIONAL TOPPINGS
Soured cream or yoghurt
Fresh coriander and/or spring
  onions, sliced
Sliced avocado
Sliced radishes or cucumber
Lime wedges
Jarred jalapeño slices or
  chilli flakes

A tomato-less chilli, hence the name 'white chilli'.
I use yellow peppers here to keep the chilli 'white' but use whatever colour you can find. I like to serve the toppings separately and let everyone help themselves. In terms of the beans, use whatever white beans you like, such as cannellini or butter beans. I find sweetcorn is always worth keeping in the freezer, but if you've got tinned sweetcorn, then drain, rinse and add it right at the end.

———————

Season the chicken thighs on both sides with salt. Heat the olive oil in a large pot and, once warm, add the chicken thighs, skin-side down. Cook for 10–12 minutes over a medium-high heat until very well browned, then turn and cook on the other side for 2–3 minutes. Lift out of the pot and set aside on a large plate.

The chicken should have given out plenty of fat but if not, add a splash of olive oil to the pot and, once warm, add the onions, peppers and a pinch of salt and pepper. Fry for about 12 minutes over a medium heat until very soft, stirring every so often. Add the garlic, fry for a minute, then add the cumin, oregano and cayenne or chilli flakes and fry for 2 minutes, stirring regularly.

Return the chicken thighs to the pot and pour in the stock. Simmer for 25 minutes, then add the beans and continue to cook for another 10 minutes.

Remove the chicken thighs once cooked through and take the meat off the bones and shred. Set aside, discarding the chicken skin if you wish. Use a potato masher or the back of your wooden spoon to crush roughly a third of the beans (this will help thicken the chilli).

Add the frozen sweetcorn, then cook for 5 minutes or so until tender. Remove from the heat, add the chicken, lime juice, plus a little zest if you like, and taste for seasoning.

Ladle into bowls and finish with the toppings you like.

Jarred salad aka Jalad

Feeds 2
Takes 10 minutes

2 handfuls of cooked quinoa or
  your fave grain
2 handfuls of cooked chickpeas
1 red pepper, roughly chopped
6 radishes and/or ¼ cucumber,
  roughly chopped
100g feta
1 handful of pomegranate seeds
1 handful of soft fresh herbs, such
  as parsley, mint, dill or coriander,
  chopped

FOR THE DRESSING
2 tbsp apple cider vinegar
4 tbsp extra virgin olive oil
1 tsp honey
Pinch of chilli flakes
Sea salt and black pepper

I've been using jars to transport salads for years, since my private cheffing days, then I saw Alice Zaslavsky brand them as jalads, i.e. jarred salads, and I fell in love with them all over again. Put the dressing at the bottom, add hearty ingredients like quinoa, rice, lentils or rice, then hardy veg and work your way up to softer, more delicate ingredients, such as herbs and salad leaves at the top. Tip out into a bowl when you get to work, toss together and voila!

―――――――――

For the dressing, simply mix all the ingredients together with a pinch of salt and pepper. Divide between two jars, then top with the quinoa, then the chickpeas, red pepper and radishes and/or cucumber.

Crumble in the feta, then top with the pomegranate seeds and herbs. Close the lids and pop them in the fridge until you're ready to head out.

Fried egg fetamole on toast

Feeds 2
Takes 15 minutes

2 eggs
Olive oil or butter, for frying
2 slices of sourdough bread

FOR THE FETAMOLE
2 large avocados, peeled
  and pitted
Juice of 2 limes
2 tbsp extra virgin olive oil
1 fresh red chilli, finely chopped
100g feta, crumbled
1 handful of fresh coriander leaves
Sea salt and black pepper

Fetamole combines two of my favourite foods: guacamole and feta. I love this on toast for a working from home lunch or a brunch with friends, or you can even make your own very easy flatbreads (see page 202). Any leftover fetamole will keep covered in the fridge for a day and you could enjoy it with crudités or with salad, or to replace the hummus in the Halloumi Hummus Grain Bowl on page 98.

———————

In a large bowl, mash the avocado flesh, then stir through the lime juice, olive oil, chilli and most of the feta (hold back some for topping). Season with salt and pepper to taste.

Fry the eggs to your liking – I like my yolks sunny side up and the whites with crispy edges. Toast the sourdough.

Spoon the fetamole onto the toast, then top with the fried eggs, the reserved feta and the coriander leaves.

Working lunches

HOW TO BUILD A...
sandwich

Veggies

If the sandwich is being packed up, choose hardier veggies or salad ingredients such as carrots, celery and radishes and leave behind the softer, more watery ones like tomatoes, cucumber and lettuce.

Cooked vs raw: I like leftover roasted veggies in a sandwich but also fresh ones too – grate fresh carrots or add roasted peppers.

The bread

Look for a bread made from just flour, water and salt, plus maybe a few flavour boosts, such as olives, herbs or cheese if you like. Check out my fast Flatbreads recipe on page 202 for a homemade bread that is truly easy, speedy and delicious, and has just four ingredients.

Stomach satisfaction

Planks of mature Cheddar, leftover roast chicken, perhaps tossed with a saucy element (see right), tinned fish or seasoned boiled eggs.

Something saucy

Hummus, pesto and chilli sauce (see pages 200–1), all of which you can jazz up with different flavour combinations to keep things interesting. See also the Whipped Feta Dip (page 210) or the Harissa Aubergine Dip on page 206. Add a pinch of ground cumin to the hummus, swap out the basil in the pesto for a different herb or blanched leafy green, and tailor the chilli sauce to your spice cupboard. Don't go overboard with the saucy element – you don't want soggy bread!

A pickly finish

Quick-pickled green chilli on page 107 or quick-pickled onions on page 80.

HOW TO BUILD A...
salad

A big veggie base

Roasted veggies (maybe rolled over from dinner the night before or made in a big batch earlier in the week), or fresh juicy veg like tomatoes, avocado or peppers or a combo. Half cooked, half raw, depending on what you fancy or the time of year.

A hearty foundation

Grains, beans, pulses or potatoes. Try new varieties – swap chickpeas or butter beans for borlotti beans, change up rice for pearl barley, freekeh or spelt. Or in a pinch, use a pouch of pre-cooked mixed grains (check the label!).

Something leafy or herby

Peppery rocket or watercress, crunchy baby gem lettuce or chicory and any fresh herbs you have in the fridge (I like to add the leaves whole, treating them like a salad leaf, and finely chop the stems – waste not, want not!).

Something crunchy

Toasted or roasted nuts or seeds (see Five-minute Frying Pan Sticky Spiced Nuts and Seeds on page 208), croutons made from stale bread or flatbreads (page 202), crumbled crackers (page 215) or crispy beans (see page 54 for crispy chickpeas – swap the chickpeas for any beans you have and swap the curry powder for whatever ground spices you like).

Finally, something creamy

A dressing (see the tahini dressing on page 46 or the hummus on page 200 or the peanut dressing on page 50), or simply sliced avocado, crumbled feta or goat's cheese, a dollop of creamy cottage cheese or yoghurt. Anything you fancy to give extra satisfaction and bring the salad together.

HOW TO BUILD A...

lunchbox

Something sustaining

For maximum satisfaction, include **protein** – **lentils, beans** (see Butter Beans and Roasted Peppers with Chimichurri on page 52), **boiled eggs** (see the Potato and Egg Salad with Purple Sprouting Broccoli on page 49) or omelette ribbons on page 85, **tinned or fresh fish** (see Herby Lentil Salad with Hot-smoked Salmon on page 56). Or a little leftover harissa **chicken** (page 108).

Something left over

Cook once, eat twice – make extra for dinner the night before, eg rice/mixed grains/lentils/quinoa and roll over into your lunchbox or a Jarred Salad aka Jalad (see page 65), where you layer your leftovers, then top with fresh leaves and final flourishes or toppings.

Something crunchy

Crunchy veg like carrots, celery, fennel, peppers and radishes. These all hold up well throughout the morning (crucial!) and are perfect for dunking into your favourite dips, which leads me on to my next lunchbox element…

Something dippy

Hummus (see page 200), or for all the feta fans out there, try the Whipped Feta Dip on page 210 or the Fetamole on page 66, which combines feta and guacamole. As well as crunchy veg for dipping, you could make a batch of the Super Seedy Crackers on page 215, or very simply slice some apples and serve with almond butter.

Something sweet

I love the Double Apple and Cinnamon Oat Bars on page 187, the Carrot Cake Oat Cookies on page 181 or Chocolate Peanut Butter (No-bake) Bars on page 182. All of these will be the crowning glory of your lunchbox.

30-minute meals

We've already talked a lot in this book about how it's often lack of time that leads us to rely so heavily on UPF-laden convenience options, so here is a whole chapter of half-hour heroes and the good news is that lots of them take well under 30 minutes.

A few of my favourites are the **Greek Salad with Crispy Oregano Potatoes** (page 92), **Speedy Sesame Stir-fried Noodles with Kimchi** (page 100) and the **Tuna, Chilli and Rocket Spaghetti** (page 95), which I deliberately make extra of togive me leftovers for lunch the next day.

And because some people worry that 30-minute recipes aren't always realistic – here are some tips to help you be as efficient as possible in the kitchen without stressing:

Use your time wisely and prep ingredients for the next step while the first step is cooking. For example, chop your other veg in the 10 minutes it takes for the onion to soften – don't try and get it all done beforehand.

Take your meat, fish and dairy out of the fridge ahead of time so they're at room temperature, which will speed up the cooking process.

Crank the oven right up at the start, so it's preheated by the time you need it. Similarly, if you need a pot of boiling water for pasta, get that on the go straight away before cracking on with everything else.

Keep all your cooking essentials by your cooker so you're not wasting time gathering everything together (my friend calls this her masterchef zone). Mine has the things I use all the time – an all-rounder knife, a chopping board and a couple of wooden spoons, as well as salt, pepper, olive oil and chilli flakes.

Hope you enjoy these half-hour heroes!

30-minute meals

DIY ciabatta pizzas

Feeds 4

Takes 30 minutes

1 large loaf of ciabatta
2 tsp dried oregano
250g mozzarella
1 handful of fresh basil leaves
Sea salt and black pepper

FOR THE TOMATO SAUCE
3 tbsp olive oil
2 garlic cloves, thinly sliced
1 x 400g tin of chopped tomatoes

OPTIONAL TOPPINGS
Pinch of chilli flakes
1 large handful of black olives
Jarred anchovies
Jarred artichokes
Jarred sun-dried tomatoes

All of the pizza joy, none of the dough faff. A great one to share with friends on a Friday night. Let everyone finish their own section of the ciabatta with their chosen toppings. Serve with a big green crunchy salad.

————————

To make the sauce, put the olive oil and garlic in a pan and fry over a medium-low heat for a couple of minutes until fragrant. Tip in the tinned tomatoes. Fill up the tin roughly a quarter of the way with water and swill it around to get all the last bits of tomato. Pour into the pan. Season with salt and pepper and simmer for 10–15 minutes until thick and reduced.

Meanwhile, prepare the ciabatta and toppings. Preheat the grill to medium-high. Slice the ciabatta in half lengthways. Grill on a tray, cut-side down, for 1–2 minutes until lightly golden, then turn and grill, cut-side up, for 1–2 minutes until lightly golden.

Taste the tomato sauce for seasoning, then spoon it over the ciabatta. Sprinkle with the oregano, tear over the mozzarella, then season the mozzarella with a little salt and pepper. Add any toppings you like, then grill for about 3–5 minutes (everyone's grill is different so keep an eye on it!) until the mozzarella is melted and lightly golden. Scatter over the basil leaves and enjoy.

Golden rice with toasted cashews, garlic yoghurt and quick-pickled red onions

Feeds 4
Takes 25 minutes

50g unsalted butter
5 cardamom pods, bashed
1 cinnamon stick
1 tsp ground turmeric
1 bay leaf
300g white basmati rice, rinsed
  and drained
500ml boiling water
100g cashews, roughly chopped
2 tbsp olive oil
4 eggs
1 large handful of fresh coriander
  leaves
Sea salt

FOR THE GARLIC YOGHURT
200g thick yoghurt
2 garlic cloves, finely chopped
  or grated
Zest of 1 lemon

FOR THE QUICK-PICKLED RED ONIONS
1 large red onion, thinly sliced
Juice of 1 lemon

A meal in itself with the crispy fried egg on top. Or serve alongside some fish or chicken. It smells incredible and looks beautiful. Though the ingredients list is a little long, as I couldn't resist the extras, it's super easy and speedy to get on the table. You can make this with brown rice but the colour from the turmeric will pop with the white rice. Any leftovers are delicious cold in a lunchbox salad the next day.

———————

Melt the butter in a medium saucepan and, once foaming, add the spices and bay leaf. Fry over a medium heat for 1–2 minutes until fragrant, then add the rice and stir to coat in the spiced butter. Add the boiling water and a pinch of salt, reduce the heat to low and cover with a tight-fitting lid. Cook for 12 minutes, then turn off the heat and leave to steam for 10 minutes.

Meanwhile, make the garlic yoghurt by mixing the ingredients in a bowl and seasoning to taste. For the quick-pickled onions, add both ingredients to a bowl with a pinch of salt and scrunch the onions to soften. Set aside to quick-pickle.

In a dry frying pan, toast the cashews over a medium-low heat for 4–5 minutes until golden. Shake the pan regularly and watch over them carefully as they can go from lovely and golden to burned quite quickly. Transfer to a bowl, then return the pan to a medium-high heat, add the olive oil and, once hot, crack in the eggs. Fry for a few minutes until the whites are set but the yolks are still runny.

Fluff up the rice with a fork and top with the toasted cashews and coriander. Serve with the garlic yoghurt, quick-pickled onions and fried eggs.

30-minute meals

Tomato salad with crispy borlotti beans

Feeds 2
Takes 25 minutes

1 x 400g tin of borlotti beans,
  drained and rinsed
2 tsp dried oregano
4 tbsp olive oil
500g large vine tomatoes (a mix of
  colours is lovely if you can find
  them), cut into big chunks
1 large handful of fresh basil leaves
Sea salt and black pepper

FOR THE ANCHOVY DRESSING
1 garlic clove, peeled
4 anchovy fillets
Pinch of dried oregano
2 tbsp red wine vinegar
4 tbsp extra virgin olive oil

Super fresh with lots of lovely basil and a punchy anchovy dressing. This is one to save for the summer months and early autumn when tomatoes are at their very best and taste most tomato-ey! A mix of colours is lovely if you can find them and if you can't find borlotti beans, pick another bean like cannellini.

───────────

Preheat the oven to fan 200°C/gas mark 7. Pat the beans dry in a clean tea towel. Spread out on a large baking tray. Toss with the oregano and olive oil, then season with salt and pepper. Roast for 10 minutes, toss, then return to the oven for another 7–10 minutes until crispy.

Meanwhile, for the dressing, use the side of your knife to smash the garlic clove. Finely chop the anchovies, then use the side of the knife to smoosh to a rough paste. Put the garlic, anchovies, oregano, vinegar, olive oil, some black pepper and a small pinch of salt (bear in mind that the anchovies are salty) in a jam jar, lid on, and shake well to emulsify.

Put the tomatoes and most of the basil (save some for serving) in a large bowl. Add half of the roasted beans and drizzle over the dressing. Toss well and taste for seasoning.

Scatter over the rest of the roasted beans and reserved basil leaves to serve.

30-minute meals

Rainbow rice
with omelette ribbons

Feeds 2
Takes 20 minutes

3 tbsp olive oil or unsalted butter
1 bunch of spring onions,
  thinly sliced
1 red or yellow pepper, thinly sliced
1 large carrot, cut into matchsticks
2 garlic cloves, finely grated
  or sliced
Thumb of fresh ginger, finely grated
150g cooked rice
1 handful of frozen edamame beans
100g kale or cabbage, thinly sliced

FOR THE OMELETTE RIBBONS
2 eggs
Knob of butter
Sea salt and black pepper

TO SERVE (OPTIONAL)
Tamari or soy sauce
Toasted sesame oil
Chilli oil or sauce (see page 201
  for homemade)
Lime wedges

This dish is nearly all in the prep – once everything is chopped and sliced, it comes together in a flash. It's best made with leftover rice but you could make rice specially for this, of course, you'll need about 50g (uncooked weight) and it's great with quinoa too. To use as many different rainbow veg as possible, I recommend frozen edamame, sweetcorn and peas (you can buy mixed bags). Make extra omelette ribbons and use them in tomorrow's lunchbox. Try making your own chilli sauce (see page 201) – it keeps well in the fridge.

———————

Start by making the omelette ribbons. Whisk the eggs with some salt and pepper. Heat a non-stick frying pan over a medium heat. Add half the butter and, once foaming, ladle in roughly half the seasoned eggs. Tilt the pan to spread thinly and evenly over the pan. Cook for a couple of minutes until just set, then slip out of the pan onto a chopping board. Repeat with the remaining butter and eggs.

Return the empty pan to the heat and add the oil or butter. Once warm/melted, add the spring onions, pepper and carrot, then season with salt and pepper. Fry over a medium-high heat for 2 minutes, then add the garlic and ginger, fry for a minute, then add the rice, edamame and kale or cabbage. Fry for 3 minutes until the rice is hot and the greens are wilted. Cut the omelettes into ribbons and either stir them through the rice or serve on top. Finish with toppings of your choice.

Peperonata pasta
(Italian pepper sauce)

Feeds 4

Takes 30 minutes

5 tbsp olive oil, plus extra
  for drizzling
2 red onions, finely sliced
4 red peppers, finely sliced
4 garlic cloves, finely sliced
Pinch of chilli flakes
1 x 400g tin of chopped tomatoes
2 tbsp capers
350g dried orzo
2–3 tbsp red wine vinegar, to taste
Sea salt and black pepper

TO SERVE
1 large handful of fresh basil leaves
Grated Parmesan

This makes enough sauce to satisfy four people generously. Even if cooking for just you or for two, I'd recommend making the full amount of sauce – it can be spooned over toast, tossed through beans or enjoyed as a base for baked eggs, shakshuka-style, or it freezes well for when you need a late-night pasta fix.

———————

Heat the olive oil in a large pot and, once warm, add the onions, peppers and a pinch of salt and pepper, Cover and cook over a medium-low heat for 15 minutes, stirring every so often. Add the garlic and chilli flakes and fry for a minute or two until fragrant, then add the tinned tomatoes and capers. Bring to the boil, then reduce to a simmer and cook (uncovered), stirring occasionally, for 15 minutes.

Meanwhile, bring a large pot of salted water to the boil and cook the orzo until al dente. Reserve a big mug of pasta water, then drain the orzo.

Taste the sauce for seasoning, adding the red wine vinegar to taste. Add the orzo, along with a splash of the reserved pasta water and toss. Serve straight away with the basil, grated Parmesan and an extra drizzle of olive oil.

Smashed broccoli
and anchovy pasta

Feeds 4
Takes 20 minutes

75g whole almonds, roughly
  chopped
6 tbsp olive oil
6 garlic cloves, finely sliced
Pinch of chilli flakes
8 anchovy fillets
2 heads of broccoli: heads cut
  into small florets, stalks cut into
  small chunks
400g dried pasta
30g Parmesan, grated, plus extra
  to serve
Juice of ½ lemon
Sea salt and black pepper

Always a crowd-pleaser, this dish has extra texture (and satisfaction) from the lovely fried almonds. The broccoli stalks are also cooked down in the sauce, they're just as important and delicious as the broccoli florets and this reduces food waste too.

———————

Put the almonds and olive oil in a large pan, set over a medium heat, and fry for 2 minutes, then add the garlic and fry for another 2 minutes until beginning to soften, but be careful the garlic doesn't brown. Add the chilli flakes and anchovies, season with black pepper, then fry until the anchovies melt into the oil.

Meanwhile, bring a large pot of salted water to the boil, then add all the broccoli. Cook for 3–4 minutes until bright green and just tender. Use a slotted spoon to lift the broccoli out of the water and transfer to the garlic, chilli and anchovy mixture. Drop the pasta into the same pot of salted water and set a timer for a couple of minutes less than the packet instructions.

Fry the broccoli for 2–3 minutes, breaking up the florets with the end of your wooden spoon until they have softened further but still retain their colour. Remove from the heat, stir in the Parmesan, little by little, followed by the lemon juice. Taste for seasoning and set aside until the pasta is done.

When the pasta is almost al dente, reserve a mug of the pasta water, then drain the pasta and tip it into the pot of broccoli. Toss well, add a splash of the reserved pasta water and continue to toss for a minute or two, adding a little more pasta water as necessary, until everything comes together. Serve straight away with extra Parmesan.

30-minute meals

Kale and brown rice bowls
with quick-pickled ginger

Feeds 2
Takes 20 minutes (45 minutes
if cooking rice)

200g cooked brown rice or
  100g uncooked brown rice
2 large handfuls of kale
2 eggs
1 small avocado, cut into
  small chunks
2 tsp sesame seeds
Sea salt

FOR THE QUICK-PICKLED GINGER
2 thumbs of fresh ginger (about
  40g), cut into thin matchsticks
4 tbsp apple cider vinegar

FOR THE DRESSING
1 tbsp miso paste
3 tbsp extra virgin olive oil
2 tbsp ginger pickling vinegar
1 tsp maple syrup
Pinch of chilli flakes, plus extra
  to serve

A healthy bowl that actually really hits the spot satisfaction-wise and is downright delicious too. Sometimes I soft-boil the eggs, sometimes I fry them until crispy, sometimes I make omelette ribbons, see page 85. You can find quite a few different varieties of miso in our shops these days. I really like white miso – it's quite subtle but adds an amazing depth of flavour. If you go for a red or brown miso, you might need a little less in the dressing as they tend to be more intensely flavoured. Use any leftover pickled ginger in noodle salads or with fried rice.

_____

If your rice isn't cooked, get that on the go according to the packet instructions. When the rice is almost cooked, drain off any excess liquid, return to the pan, put the kale on top of the rice, put the lid on and leave to steam for 10 minutes until the kale is tender. If using pre-cooked rice, simply reheat the rice until piping hot and steam the kale for a few minutes until bright green and tender.

For the quick-pickled ginger, put the ginger, vinegar and a pinch of salt in a bowl. Toss well and set aside for 15 minutes as you prepare the rest of the bowls.

Boil the eggs in salted water for 6–8 minutes, depending on whether you like a soft-, medium- or hard-boiled egg. Run under cold water to stop the eggs cooking, then peel.

Meanwhile, make the dressing by simply whisking all the ingredients together in a small bowl.

Put the rice and kale in bowls. Drizzle over the dressing, then top with the avocado chunks, the halved eggs and some quick-pickled ginger. Serve with extra chilli flakes and the sesame seeds.

30-minute meals

Greek salad with crispy oregano potatoes

Feeds 2

Takes 30 minutes

100g feta, roughly chopped
  or crumbled
200g tomatoes, chopped (or halved
  if small)
½ cucumber, chopped
1 pepper (any colour), chopped
2 handfuls of olives, halved and
  pitted (I like black Kalamata ones)
½ small red onion, finely chopped
  (optional)
1 handful of soft fresh herbs, such
  as mint, flat-leaf parsley and/or dill,
  roughly chopped

FOR THE POTATOES
3 potatoes (about 400g), chopped
  lengthways into 2.5cm chips
3 tbsp olive oil
1 tsp dried oregano
Sea salt and black pepper

FOR THE DRESSING
3 tbsp extra virgin olive oil
Juice of 1 lemon
Pinch of dried oregano

Two of my favourite orders on a Greek island (or in a Greek restaurant in London) are the feta salad and the chips. I can't master their insanely good chips in my home kitchen, but this version still hits the spot when I get the craving, as this feels like sunshine food. Look out for mixed colours of tomatoes and peppers to enjoy a variety of plants.

———————

Preheat the oven to fan 220°C/gas mark 9. Toss the potatoes with the olive oil, oregano, and some salt and pepper. Bake for 30 minutes, tossing after 20 minutes, until golden brown and crispy at the edges.

Meanwhile, mix all the dressing ingredients together in a large bowl and season to taste with salt and pepper. Toss through all of the salad ingredients.

Spoon the salad over the crispy oregano potatoes and enjoy straight away.

Tuna, chilli and rocket spaghetti

Feeds 2
Takes 20 minutes

200g dried spaghetti
4 tbsp olive oil, plus extra
  for drizzling
3 garlic cloves, finely sliced
1 large courgette, coarsely grated
1 red chilli, finely chopped (or big
  pinch of chilli flakes)
160g tinned tuna (drained weight,
  about 2 tins)
2 large handfuls of rocket
Zest and juice of ½ lemon
Sea salt and black pepper
Chilli flakes, to serve (optional)

We call this Tuesday Night Tuna in our house. It's a perfect solution on those midweek nights when time is running away with you and you need dinner to happen in a flash. The sauce comes together in the time it takes the pasta to cook. Sardines are a delicious option too, and a great way to get some more omega-3 oily fish in. Choose responsibly sourced fish when you can. If your tuna comes packed in olive oil, use some of this for frying the garlic and chilli. Waste not, want not!

————————

Bring a large pot of salted water to the boil, then add the spaghetti and set a timer for a couple of minutes less than the packet instructions.

Meanwhile, put the olive oil and garlic in a large pot and cook over a medium-low heat for a couple of minutes until fragrant and softened but not browned. Add the grated courgette and the chilli (or chilli flakes), then season with salt and pepper and cook for a couple of minutes until softened. Remove from the heat and stir through the tuna and rocket. Set aside until the pasta is ready.

When the pasta is almost al dente, reserve a big mug of the pasta water, then drain the pasta. Add the spaghetti to the tuna mixture. Over a medium heat, toss everything together to wilt the rocket and emulsify the sauce. Add splashes of the reserved pasta water, as needed. Stir through the lemon zest and juice, taste for seasoning, then serve with an extra drizzle of olive and some chilli flakes if you like more heat.

Miso mushrooms on toast

Feeds 2

Takes 25 minutes

4 tbsp olive oil, plus extra (optional)
  for drizzling
400g mixed mushrooms, roughly
  chopped or torn
1 tbsp apple cider vinegar
2 tbsp miso paste (I use white
  miso)
1–2 tbsp warm water
2 garlic cloves, finely chopped
1 handful of finely chopped
  fresh chives
2 slices of toast
Shavings or gratings of Parmesan
  or Cheddar (optional)

Super savoury from both the mushrooms and miso, making it a very satisfying (not to mention speedy) meal. The mushroom mixture is also delicious tossed through pasta and it's a good time to try some different varieties – my faves are shiitake and chestnut. Different types cook at slightly different rates, so since you're frying in two batches (this prevents the pan from overcrowding – no one wants a soggy mushroom), cook varieties that cook at a similar rate together. Sometimes, I'll add a few eggs on top, usually fried eggs.

———————

Heat 2 tablespoons of the olive oil in a large frying pan and, once hot, add half the mushrooms and fry over a medium-high heat for 8–10 minutes until well browned, all the liquid has cooked out and the mushrooms are golden at the edges. Remove from the pan and repeat with the remaining 2 tablespoons of olive oil and the rest of the mushrooms.

Meanwhile, in a small bowl, mix the vinegar, miso and warm water together to reach a drizzling consistency.

Return the first batch of mushrooms to the pan along with the garlic. Fry for a minute or two until fragrant, then remove from the heat and pour in the miso mixture. Use a wooden spoon to scrape up any sticky bits from the pan and stir to coat the mushrooms with the miso mixture. Stir in most of the chives and then spoon onto the toasts. Top with the remaining chives, plus an extra drizzle of olive oil and cheese on top, if you like.

Halloumi hummus grain bowl

Feeds 4
Takes 20 minutes

250g cooked quinoa or other grain
  (see intro)
2 boiled eggs, peeled and halved
  (cooked for about 7 minutes)
Hummus (see page 200
  for homemade)
Juice of 1 lemon
Extra virgin olive oil, for drizzling
Sea salt and black pepper

FOR THE HALLOUMI
2 tbsp olive oil
225g halloumi, patted dry and cut
  into 8 slices

PICK YOUR OWN ELEMENTS
Chopped tomatoes, cucumber,
  peppers or cabbage
Chopped fresh herbs, lettuce
  or onion
A little sauerkraut, pickles or kimchi

Once a week, I cook up a batch of grains and change it up each week, for example, quinoa, rice, pearl barley, mixed grains or Puy lentils. I've then got an amazing base for salads for lunch or dinner. While you're at it, you could also prepare some boiled eggs to keep in the fridge and a batch of homemade hummus (see page 200). Plastic pots of shop-bought hummus are all too easy to grab, but it really is easy and affordable to make at home and just one tin of chickpeas will give you hummus to last the week. This recipe is colourful, so it feels special, but it's still simple enough for when friends come over as it's very much a DIY, help yourself, build your own bowl. Plus, it's vegetarian (do check the halloumi is veggie, as some is made with animal rennet) and satisfies everyone. If you want to take this for a packed lunch, then swap the fried halloumi for feta or goat's cheese, so you can skip frying the halloumi.

For the halloumi, heat the olive oil in a large frying pan. Once hot, add the halloumi slices and fry over a high heat for 1–2 minutes on each side until golden.

Assemble the bowls with the grains, veg, herbs and pickles of your choice, the boiled eggs, hummus and halloumi, seasoning with the lemon juice, olive oil and some salt and pepper.

Speedy sesame stir-fried noodles with kimchi

Feeds 2
Takes 20 minutes

150g your fave noodles
2 tbsp coconut oil or olive oil
1 bunch of spring onions, quartered
2 handfuls of green beans, halved
2 heads of pak choi or 2 handfuls
  of cabbage, finely sliced
1 handful of frozen edamame beans
1 handful of sesame seeds (black
  or white or a mix)
Sea salt
Kimchi, to serve

FOR THE SAUCE
2 tbsp runny tahini
3 tbsp soy sauce or tamari, or more
  to taste
½ garlic clove, finely chopped
2 tsp toasted sesame oil
1 tbsp apple cider vinegar or mirin
2 tsp maple syrup or honey

When I visited Seoul in South Korea, I loved the food so much that, on a few occasions, I had two dinners as I couldn't resist the late-night noodle spots. Everyone needs a late-night noodle recipe up their sleeve. This is a sesame three-ways recipe – you've got the toasted sesame oil, the tahini (sesame seed paste) and the sesame seeds on top. When you're looking out for kimchi in the shops, you want the properly fermented type with live bacteria, so look for the kind in the refrigerated section and store it in the fridge when you get home.

_____

For the sauce, simply whisk all the ingredients together in a bowl or shake in a jam jar. Taste for seasoning and adjust with a little more soy or tamari or sea salt. The rest of the garlic clove can be added to the vegetable stir-fry. If your tahini is thick, add a tablespoon or two of water to loosen.

In a saucepan, cook the noodles in salted boiling water according to the packet instructions. Drain and toss with the sauce and then divide between two bowls.

Meanwhile, in a large pan, heat the oil, then add the spring onions, green beans, pak choi or cabbage and edamame and stir-fry over a medium-high heat for 5–8 minutes until tender. Add to the bowls, scatter over the sesame seeds and add a spoonful of kimchi.

Traybakes

I love a traybake. A bit of chopping and then you can let the oven do all the work for you, while leaving you with hardly any washing up. There's nothing better for those midweek evenings when you don't have the energy to cook and you just want to fall onto the sofa.

I have two pieces of advice: firstly, **choose your largest tray**. Spreading ingredients out on a large, low-sided tray allows them to roast rather than steam, meaning you get lovely crispy edges and lots of flavour from caramelisation. Most of the recipes in this chapter serve two but can be scaled up to feed more people; if you're scaling up, I'd suggest using two large baking trays and rotating them from the top shelf to the lower shelf and vice versa about two-thirds of the way through the cook times. You may need to give them an extra 5–10 minutes in the oven to make up for the extra volume/quantities of ingredients – just keep an eye out for when everything starts to look golden and gorgeous.

The only exception to the large, low-sided baking tray recommendation is when you're adding liquid to the tray (such as in the **Coconut Cauliflower Traybake** on page 107), in which case you'll want to choose a baking tray with high sides to avoid a messy saucy situation!

The second piece of advice is layering. By this I mean, **adding the ingredients into the tray depending on the length of time it takes for them to cook**. For example, I'd give any root veggies like carrots, beetroot and potatoes a head start before adding ingredients that cook relatively quickly like fish or greens. Just don't forget to season each layer as you go to really amplify the flavour of the end result. For more tips, check out **How to Build a Traybake** on pages 126–7 and let that inspire your own traybake adventures.

Coconut cauliflower traybake with quick-pickled green chillies

Feeds 2

Takes 1 hour (lots of hands-off time)

2 tbsp coconut oil

1 cauliflower

1 brown onion, cut through the root into 6 wedges

4 garlic cloves, unpeeled

Thumb of fresh ginger, finely chopped

2 tsp medium curry powder

1 x 400g tin of chickpeas, drained and rinsed

1 x 400ml tin of full-fat coconut milk

Sea salt and black pepper

FOR THE QUICK-PICKLED GREEN CHILLIES

1 green chilli, thinly sliced

Juice of 1 lime

DELICIOUS WITH:

Flatbreads (see page 202), naan and/or rice

I've always loved cauliflower in curries. This traybake is an easy way to get a hands-off beautifully flavoured and warming spiced veggie dinner. Pickled green chillies give nice brightness to the coconutty richness, but red chillies work just as well. Deseed the chillies if you don't fancy too much of a kick.

———————

To make the quick pickled chillies, mix the sliced chilli, lime juice and a pinch of salt in a small bowl. Set aside to quick-pickle as you get on with everything else.

Preheat the oven to fan 200°C/gas mark 7 while you put the coconut oil in a large roasting tray (one with sides, as you'll be adding in coconut milk later) and pop it in the oven to melt as the oven comes up to temperature.

Trim the cauliflower and remove any especially tough outer leaves but leave on the paler green, thinner leaves. Cut into quarters through the root. Add the cauliflower wedges, onion wedges, garlic cloves, ginger and curry powder to the roasting tray containing the melted coconut oil. Season with salt and pepper and toss really well so that everything is nicely coated. Roast for 15 minutes, then remove the tray and pour the chickpeas and coconut milk into the base of the tray (try to avoid the cauliflower as you want the tops to stay dry so they go crispy). Fill the empty coconut milk tin a quarter of the way up with water, swill the water around to get every last bit and add this to the tray too. Return to the oven for another 25 minutes or so until the tops of the cauliflower wedges are crispy and lightly charred and all the veg is tender.

Serve by topping the cauli with the quick-pickled chillies, along with all the chilli-lime juice for spooning over, with your choice of flatbreads, naan and/or rice alongside.

Harissa chicken with potato wedges, roasted lemons and spring onions

Feeds 2
Takes 45 minutes

4 bone-in, skin-on chicken thighs
  (about 600g)
400g potatoes, cut into wedges
3 tbsp olive oil
1 bunch of spring onions,
  roughly chopped
Sea salt and black pepper
Chopped cucumber and herb
  (flat-leaf parsley, coriander, dill
  or mint) salad, to serve

FOR THE SAUCE
2 tbsp+ rose harissa paste, to taste
2 tbsp yoghurt
Zest of 1 lemon

This is always on a fortnightly rotation round mine.
I like to double up the recipe and spread it over a
second baking tray, so I've got extras to stuff into
a sandwich for lunch for the week or I toss the
leftovers with lettuce and avocado to make a big
5-minute lunchbox salad. Delicious.

———————

For the sauce, simply mix the ingredients together in a
large mixing bowl and season with a generous pinch of
salt and pepper. Add the chicken thighs to the bowl and
toss to coat the chicken. If you have time, you could do this
in advance and store in the fridge for up to 24 hours, but I
never remember to.

Preheat the oven to fan 200°C/gas mark 7. Put the potatoes
into your largest roasting tray. Cut the lemon you zested
for the sauce into 4 wedges and add them too. Drizzle with
2 tablespoons of the olive oil, season with salt and pepper,
toss well, then spread out evenly. Lay the chicken thighs on
top, then drizzle with the final tablespoon of olive oil.

Roast for 20 minutes, then add the spring onions, toss
to coat in the oily cooking juices and return to the oven
for another 10–15 minutes until the chicken and potatoes
are golden and tender. (You can add the spring onions
at the start to skip a step but they can get quite dark and
crispy, whereas I like it when they keep their colour and
just soften.)

Serve straight from the roasting tray with the herby
cucumber salad and the roasted lemon wedges for
squeezing over.

Herby cod, cherry tomatoes, olives and lentils

Feeds 2
Takes 25 minutes

300g cherry tomatoes
1 small handful of fresh oregano
 or thyme leaves or 1 tsp dried
About 5 tbsp olive oil
1 x 400g tin of lentils, drained
 and rinsed
100g kale or cavolo nero, leaves
 stripped and roughly chopped
 or torn
1 large handful of pitted (green)
 olives
2 fillets of cod, patted dry
2 tbsp fresh pesto (see page 200
 for homemade)
Sea salt and black pepper
1 lemon, cut into wedges, to serve

An easy effortless traybake inspired by late summer holidays to the south of France. Kale and lentils are often promoted as being so good for us but aren't always up there with everyone's cravings – here they are paired with sweet juicy cherry tomatoes, rich olives and pesto. Change up your fish here – try hake or pollock if you prefer. Or for ease, use frozen cod that you have defrosted and patted dry (frozen fish tends to be more 'wet', so don't skip that step!).

———————

Preheat the oven to fan 180°C/gas mark 6. Put the tomatoes, oregano and 2 tablespoons of the olive oil in a large roasting tray. Season with salt and pepper, toss well, then bake for 10 minutes. Lift out the tomatoes and scatter the lentils into the tray. Stir through the kale and top with the tomatoes, olives and cod fillets.

Season the cod with salt and pepper and drizzle with 2 tablespoons of the olive oil. Bake for 8–12 minutes (depending on the thickness of your fillets) until the fish flakes easily when pressed lightly with a fork.

Loosen the pesto with the remaining tablespoon of olive oil, or more if necessary, to reach a drizzling consistency. Drizzle the pesto over the traybake and serve with lemon wedges.

Ginger spring onion salmon

Feeds 2

Takes 25 minutes

250g new potatoes, halved or
   quartered if large
3 tbsp olive oil
250g Tenderstem or purple
   sprouting broccoli
2 firm fish fillets, such as
   wild salmon
Sea salt and black pepper

FOR THE GINGER SPRING ONION
   DRIZZLE
1 bunch of spring onions,
   very thinly sliced
Thumb of fresh ginger (about 20g),
   finely grated
Zest and juice of 1 lemon
Pinch of chilli flakes
4 tbsp olive oil

A super speedy traybake. Make sure you also use the green parts of the spring onions in the drizzle, which comes together quickly while everything else is roasting away. If you're using a regular head of broccoli, just make sure the florets are chopped small so that they cook in time. When in season, asparagus would be lovely here too.

———————

Preheat the oven to fan 200°C/gas mark 7. Toss the potatoes with 2 tablespoons of the olive oil and some salt and pepper. Spread out on a roasting tray and roast for 15 minutes until just starting to turn golden.

Meanwhile, make the drizzle by mixing together all the ingredients (except for a small handful of sliced spring onions to serve). Season to taste.

Toss the potatoes on the tray, then add the broccoli and salmon fillets, spreading everything out as best you can. Drizzle the broccoli with the remaining tablespoon of olive oil and season. Spoon roughly half the ginger spring onion drizzle over the salmon. Roast for a further 8–10 minutes until the salmon is just cooked through (it should flake easily and still be juicy).

Serve with the rest of the drizzle and sprinkle over the reserved spring onions.

Aubergine, cherry tomato and butter bean traybake

Feeds 2

Takes 35 minutes

2 small red onions, cut through the
  root into wedges
1 large aubergine, cut into
  2.5cm pieces
5 tbsp olive oil
2 tsp dried oregano
400g cherry tomatoes
1 x 400g tin of butter beans,
  drained and rinsed, or ½ x 660g
  jar of butter beans, drained
100g feta
1 large handful of rocket or
  watercress
Pinch of chilli flakes (optional)
Sea salt and black pepper

This tastes like summer! Aubergines and tomatoes are my fave pasta combination and here they are combined with hearty beans – butter beans in particular are satisfyingly gorgeous in this. I love how the feta contrasts with the traybake, but if you want those Pasta alla Norma vibes, then use a veg peeler to peel over shavings of pecorino cheese to serve.

———————

Preheat the oven to fan 220°C/gas mark 9.

Toss the onions and aubergine pieces with 3 tablespoons of the olive oil, the oregano, and some salt and pepper. Spread out on a large baking tray and roast for 15 minutes until turning lightly golden. Add the cherry tomatoes and butter beans, drizzle with the remaining 2 tablespoons of olive oil, season and return to the oven for 15 minutes until the beans are slightly crisped up and all the veg is tender.

Slice or crumble over the feta and scatter over the rocket or watercress and chilli flakes, if using. Serve straight from the tray and enjoy!

Spiced squash and crispy chickpea traybake with tahini drizzle

Feeds 2

Takes 45 minutes

½ *small butternut squash,*
  deseeded and cut into
  large wedges
5 *tbsp olive oil*
1 *tbsp ground spices, such as ras*
  el hanout (see intro)
2 *red onions, each one cut through*
  the root into 8 wedges
1 *x 400g tin of chickpeas, drained,*
  rinsed and patted dry
2 *large handfuls of roughly torn kale*
1 *handful of pomegranate seeds*
Sea salt and black pepper

FOR THE TAHINI DRIZZLE
2 *tbsp tahini (stirred well in the*
  jar first)
1 *tbsp apple cider vinegar*

With its natural sweetness, squash can take on a good dose of warming spices. I love butternut squash and it tends to be the most widely available, but use any squash or pumpkin you like the look of. Ras el hanout, the key ingredient in delicious Moroccan tagines, is available in most shops. If you can't find it, make your own homemade ras el hanout-style spice mix with ½ teaspoon each of ground coriander, cumin, cinnamon, turmeric and chilli powder.

———————

Preheat the oven to fan 220°C/gas mark 9.

Put the squash wedges on a large baking tray, toss with 2 tablespoons of the olive oil, half the ras el hanout and season with salt. Roast for 15 minutes, then add the onions and chickpeas. Toss the onions and chickpeas with 2 tablespoons of the olive oil, the remaining ras el hanout and some salt. Return the tray to the oven for 20 minutes. Finally, add the kale to the tray, drizzle with the last tablespoon of olive oil and roast for 3–5 minutes until tender and slightly charred at the edges. At this point, the squash and onions should be golden and tender and the chickpeas should be crisp.

For the tahini drizzle, simply mix the tahini and vinegar in a small bowl to combine, then slowly whisk in 1–2 tablespoons of water to reach a drizzling consistency. Season to taste.

To serve, scatter the pomegranate seeds over the traybake and drizzle with the tahini sauce.

Green gnocchi traybake

Feeds 2
Takes 30 minutes

1 courgette, chopped into
   bite-sized chunks
200g gnocchi
5 tbsp olive oil
1 tsp dried oregano
1 head of broccoli, cut into
   bite-sized florets, stalk cut into
   small chunks
2 handfuls of green olives, pitted
Pinch of chilli flakes
1 handful of grated or shaved
   Parmesan
Sea salt and black pepper

FOR THE HERBY DRIZZLE
2 tbsp fresh pesto (see page 200
   for homemade)
2 tbsp extra virgin olive oil
Squeeze of lemon juice

Gnocchi is an easy, convenient food to keep in the fridge to form the base of quick meals. I like the fresh ones that you can find in the refrigerated sections of shops. If you'd like to, swap the gnocchi for halved new potatoes or small potatoes which can cook in 20 minutes along with the green veg. Look out for (preferably fresh) pesto sauces that have minimal ingredients or make your own (see page 200), swapping the almonds for pine nuts, hazelnuts or seeds, and switching the basil for blanched greens like kale or cavolo nero in the winter.

———————

Preheat the oven to fan 220°C/gas mark 9.

Put the courgette chunks and gnocchi on your largest baking tray. You want everything to be spread out with room to roast rather than steam, so use two trays if necessary and swap the oven shelf they're on halfway through roasting. Drizzle over 3 tablespoons of the olive oil and season with salt, pepper and the oregano. Roast for 15 minutes, then add the broccoli and olives, drizzle with the remaining 2 tablespoons of olive oil, season and return to the oven for a further 10 minutes until the veg is golden and the gnocchi are crispy.

Meanwhile, make the herby drizzle by simply mixing all the ingredients together in a small bowl and seasoning to taste with salt and pepper.

Drizzle the herby mixture over the gnocchi and veg. Sprinkle with chilli flakes and scatter over the Parmesan.

Sweet potato, halloumi and chickpea traybake

Feeds 2
Takes 30 minutes

2 sweet potatoes (about 350g),
   cut into wedges
1 x 400g tin of chickpeas, drained,
   rinsed and patted dry
1 tsp crushed cumin seeds or
   ground cumin
1 tsp crushed coriander seeds
   or ground coriander
5 tbsp olive oil
225g halloumi, cut into chunks
   and patted dry
1 small fennel bulb, thinly sliced
2 handfuls of pea shoots,
   watercress or your favourite
   salad leaves
Juice of ½ lemon
Sea salt and black pepper

Lots of veg all in one tray (bonus plant points if you can get your hands on purple sweet potatoes!), all lovely and caramelised with salty halloumi chunks. Serve with yoghurt and fresh pea shoots (which always work well with halloumi), but you could swap these for another soft fresh herb like coriander or parsley. If I have friends coming over, I like to make this with flatbreads (see page 202 to make your own). To warm the flatbreads, pop them in the oven for the last minute of the traybake's cooking time.

———————

Preheat the oven to fan 200°C/gas mark 7. Toss the sweet potatoes and chickpeas with the cumin and coriander, 3 tablespoons of the olive oil and a generous pinch of salt and pepper. Spread out on a large baking tray and roast for 15 minutes until just starting to turn golden.

Toss the halloumi chunks with the remaining 2 tablespoons of olive oil, then add them to the baking tray. Return to the oven for 10 minutes until the halloumi is golden at the edges and the sweet potato is tender and caramelised.

Scatter over the sliced fennel and pea shoots, and squeeze over the lemon juice to serve.

Grated halloumi toasts with hot honey

Feeds 2
Takes 20 minutes

400g cherry tomatoes
1 big handful of black olives, pitted
2 large slices of sourdough bread
3 tbsp olive oil
225g halloumi, coarsely grated
1 tsp dried oregano or thyme
Good pinch of chilli flakes
1 tbsp runny honey
2 large handfuls of rocket
Sea salt and black pepper

This recipe takes cheese on toast to the next level. As a long-term halloumi lover, it's taken me far too long to get into grating my halloumi. It's game changing. Salty golden halloumi with hot honey and its chilli kick are an amazing pairing. If you can find cherry tomatoes on the vine, they're great here.

———————

Preheat the oven to fan 220°C/gas mark 9. Put the tomatoes, olives and bread on a large baking tray. Drizzle the tomatoes with 2 tablespoons of the olive oil and season with salt and pepper. Bake for 5–7 minutes to lightly toast the bread.

Pile the grated halloumi onto the toasts, sprinkle with the oregano or thyme, drizzle with the remaining olive oil and bake for a further 10–12 minutes until the halloumi is melted and golden. As soon as you take them out of the oven, sprinkle the toasts with the chilli flakes and drizzle with the honey. Scatter over the rocket and serve straight away.

Fish and potato traybake with mojo verde and fennel salad

Feeds 2
Takes 35 minutes

250g new potatoes, halved
1 tsp dried or chopped fresh
  oregano or thyme
3 tbsp olive oil
2 fillets of sea bass, or similar
  white fish
Sea salt and black pepper

FOR THE MOJO VERDE
1 large handful of fresh
  coriander leaves
1 large handful of fresh
  parsley leaves
1 garlic clove, peeled
1 green chilli
Juice of 1 lemon
5 tbsp extra virgin olive oil

FOR THE FENNEL SALAD
1 shallot or ½ red onion,
  finely sliced
2 tbsp red wine vinegar
1 small fennel bulb, thinly sliced,
  plus the fronds if possible
3 tbsp extra virgin olive oil

A simple Spanish-inspired traybake with the famous mojo verde, a herby sauce, which my friend, the chef Kitty Coles, taught me on holiday in Mallorca. It is amazing on fish, with roast veg or baked chicken. Fish and fennel are a match made in heaven but if you've got your hands on ripe summer tomatoes, use the same salad recipe and swap the fennel for a large handful of fresh tomatoes.

———————

Preheat the oven to fan 180°C/gas mark 6. Toss the potatoes with the herbs and 2 tablespoons of the olive oil, then season with salt and pepper. Spread out on a large baking tray and roast for 20–25 minutes until golden.

Meanwhile, make the mojo verde by simply blitzing all the ingredients in a food processor until smooth and seasoning to taste. For the fennel salad, put the sliced shallot or onion and the vinegar in a bowl, season with salt and set aside for 5 minutes – this will take away the strong raw onion flavour. After 5 minutes, add the fennel slices and fronds, if using, to the bowl, toss, then drizzle in the olive oil and taste for seasoning.

Add the fish fillets to the baking tray, season with salt and pepper and drizzle with the remaining tablespoon of olive oil. Roast for 8–12 minutes, depending on the thickness of your fillets, until the fish flakes easily.

Serve the fish and potatoes with the mojo verde sauce and fennel salad.

Traybakes

HOW TO BUILD A...
traybake

Something hearty

Jarred or tinned chickpeas, beans or lentils, potatoes, sweet potatoes, squash. Use these as the base as they often need a head start in the oven.

Be sure that your ingredients are well dried, particularly washed veg and drained tinned chickpeas, as otherwise they will steam and not roast.

Lots of veggies

Get in at least two different veggies and think about different textures and colours for maximum enjoyment and goodness.

The vessel

Your largest tray. Spread out everything so that it roasts rather than steams. If you don't have a large baking/roasting tray, then two medium trays are your best bet.

Something satisfying

Chicken thighs, fish fillets, feta, halloumi, or tofu chunks for a vegan alternative.

A fat

Olive oil, coconut oil, ghee or butter.

Seasoning

Sea salt and black pepper and perhaps half a lemon in the tray to squeeze over at the end. Or your favourite ground spice mix – try harissa paste, ras el hanout or a medium curry powder.

Something creamy or cheesy

A dollop of hummus, yoghurt or soured cream, a drizzle of kefir, a crumble of feta, or tear over some goat's cheese or mozzarella or grate over some hard cheese to finish. Alternatively, add the cheese towards the end of cooking and turn the grill to high for the last 5 minutes until the cheese is golden and bubbling.

Something fresh to finish and brighten

Fresh herbs, a lovely herby drizzle, or tomato and cucumber salsa or some pickles. Or throw on some rocket, watercress or baby spinach. You could add these at the table as the final flourish. See the mojo verde on page 124, the chimichurri on page 212 or pesto on page 200.

One-pot

Who doesn't love a reliable, effortless one-pot wonder? There's a reason one-pot cooking is so popular – less faff, less washing up and you can often chuck everything in and leave it to bubble away while you get on with something else. I find them to be a real saviour during busy weeks.

When it comes to one-pot cooking, it's important to think about layering flavour and texture. For flavour, start with a strong base like onions, garlic, spices and/or herbs. From there you can build using proteins, grains and pulses and amp up flavour with pastes (the ones I use most often are tomato purée, miso and harissa). Finally, you'll need some sort of liquid (stock, tinned tomatoes and/or coconut milk). Head to page 153 to make your own stock or if you buy it from the shops, check the label for any unwanted ingredients. If you're going to finish with any leafy greens, these get added at the end so they retain their lovely colour and flavour. See more on **How to Build a Soup** on pages 154–5.

When it comes to texture, this might be in the form of crispy toppings (like the layered potatoes on the **Shepherd's Pie** on page 150), cheesy toppings (like the gooey mozzarella on the **Puttanesca Bean Gratin** on page 147), or toppings that go directly on the plates or bowls when you serve (like the avocado and quick-pickled red onions in the **Tomato Black Bean Broth** on page 140). At the end, I find a simple squeeze of lime or lemon juice is often all you need to lift your finished dish.

One-pot dishes can also be great 'cook once, eat twice' options, as it's usually as simple as just doubling the ingredients to ensure you've got leftovers – leaving you with a nutritious dinner and lunch ready to take to work with you the next day.

Lemony lentil carrot soup

Feeds 8
Takes 30 minutes

4 tbsp olive oil
2 large onions, finely chopped
2 large carrots, chopped
4 garlic cloves, finely chopped
2 tbsp ground cumin
750g split red lentils, rinsed
   and drained
2.5 litres vegetable stock
500ml just-boiled water (optional)
Juice of 2 lemons
Sea salt and black pepper

OPTIONAL TOPPINGS
Chilli flakes
Chopped fresh herbs or 1 handful
   of salad leaves
Greek yoghurt
Drizzle of extra virgin olive oil

Red lentils are one of the best lentils for speedy suppers as they cook to perfection in about 15 minutes. This makes enough to feed eight people and freezes well, but you can halve the recipe if you prefer. Either blitz until smooth and silky, keep it chunky, or blitz just some so that you have creaminess but still retain some texture.

———————

Heat the olive oil in your largest pan and add the onions, carrots and a pinch of salt. Fry over a medium heat for 10 minutes until soft, then stir in the garlic and cumin and fry for another minute.

Add the lentils and stock, pop the lid on and simmer for 15 minutes until the lentils are tender, stirring halfway through to ensure the lentils don't stick on the bottom.

If you prefer it smooth, add the just-boiled water and the lemon juice and blitz. If it's still a little thick, add a splash more water until you reach your desired thickness.

If you'd like to keep it chunky, simply add the lemon juice and taste for seasoning.

Serve with any of the optional toppings.

One-pot

Cosy spiced rice soup with yoghurt, pomegranate and herbs

Feeds 4
Takes 40 minutes

4 tbsp olive oil, plus extra to serve
2 onions, finely chopped
2 celery sticks, finely chopped
100g basmati rice
4 garlic cloves, finely chopped
1 tbsp ground cumin
1 tbsp ground coriander
1 tsp ground cinnamon
1 tsp ground turmeric
1 tsp paprika
2 tbsp tomato purée
½ small butternut squash
(about 300g once peeled and
deseeded), cut into small cubes
1.3 litres vegetable or chicken stock
Zest and juice of 1 lemon
Sea salt and black pepper

TO SERVE
Yoghurt or kefir
Pomegranate seeds
Fresh herbs

Inspired by a Syrian-style pilaf, this is a soup-y cosy version. I know some people don't love the idea of soup in the evening, but this beautiful hearty version is special enough for dinner, especially with the fresh herbs on top – mint, parsley or coriander leaves are perfect here. If you have any leftover cooked chicken, you could add it at the end of cooking to heat through.

———————

Set a large pot over a medium heat, add the olive oil and, once warm, add the onions, celery and a pinch of salt. Cook for 12–15 minutes, stirring every so often, until soft.

Meanwhile, rinse the rice until the water runs clear.

Add the garlic to the onions and celery. Fry for a couple of minutes, then add the spices and fry for a minute or two until fragrant, stirring constantly. Add the tomato purée, fry for 2–3 minutes until brick red, stirring constantly to prevent it from catching.

Add the squash and stir to coat in the spiced onion mixture, then pour in the stock. Bring to the boil, then reduce to a strong simmer and cook, covered, for 5 minutes. Add the rice and cook for another 10–12 minutes until the squash and rice are tender. Add the lemon zest and juice and taste for seasoning.

Serve with yoghurt or kefir, pomegranate seeds, fresh herbs and a good drizzle of olive oil.

One-pot

Golden chicken soup
with barley

Feeds 4
Takes 1 hour

4 bone-in, skin-on chicken thighs
2 tbsp olive oil, plus extra if needed
1 large onion, finely chopped
2 celery sticks, finely chopped
4 carrots, roughly chopped
2 fat garlic cloves, finely chopped
1 tsp ground turmeric
Pinch of chilli flakes, plus extra
   (optional) to serve
4 large handfuls of pearl barley
1.2 litres chicken stock
1 large handful of soft fresh herbs,
   such as parsley, dill or coriander,
   roughly chopped
3 spring onions, finely sliced
1 lime or lemon, cut into wedges
Sea salt and black pepper

Don't make me pick a favourite, but this one truly is a recipe I regularly make all year round. Pearl barley has the ideal amount of chewiness, tenderness and heartiness, and is a bit more of an old-fashioned grain, so let's bring it back. You could swap it for brown rice if you can't get your hands on pearl barley.

———————

Season the chicken thighs all over with salt and pepper. Heat the olive oil in a large pot and, once warm, add the chicken thighs, skin-side down, and fry undisturbed over a medium heat for 10–12 minutes until the skin is golden. Turn and fry for 5 minutes, then transfer to a plate.

The pot should have enough fat in it, but if not add a little more olive oil. Add the onion, celery and a pinch of salt and fry over a medium heat for 10 minutes, stirring every so often, until soft and golden. Add the carrots, garlic, turmeric and chilli flakes and fry for a couple of minutes until fragrant. Add the chicken thighs back to the pot, then add the pearl barley and pour in the stock. Bring to a simmer, pop the lid on and cook for 25 minutes until the chicken is cooked through. Remove the chicken from the pot and leave to rest and cool on a plate. Leave the soup on the heat, allowing the barley to cook for another 10 minutes until tender.

Once the chicken is just cool enough to handle, pull apart the meat into bite-sized chunks (discard the bones, and the skin if you wish) and return to the pot. Stir in the herbs and taste and adjust the seasoning.

Lade into bowls and top with the spring onions, squeeze over the lime or lemon juice and finish with extra chilli flakes if you like.

Sausage, leek and potato stew

Feeds 4

Takes 50 minutes

6 good-quality pork or veggie
  sausages
3–4 tbsp olive oil
2 large leeks, cut into bite-sized
  rounds
2 celery sticks, diced
500g potatoes, cut into bite-sized
  chunks
4 garlic cloves, sliced
2 tbsp tomato purée
1 litre chicken or vegetable stock
1 x 400g tin of white beans, drained
  and rinsed
1 tbsp Dijon or wholegrain mustard
4 large handfuls of sliced greens,
  such as cabbage, spring greens
  or cavolo nero
Chilli flakes, for sprinkling (optional)
Sea salt and black pepper

A super comforting one-pot stew that feels slow cooked but takes under an hour. Leek and potatoes are best buddies but swap leeks for onions if you can't get leeks. Use veggie sausages if you prefer and if you want to increase the diversity of vegetables, include a mix of potatoes and squash or even celeriac chunks if you like. Use any beans you like, I prefer butter or cannellini beans here.

————————

Remove the sausage meat from the casings, pull each sausage apart into four chunks and briefly mould into meatball-type shapes.

Add 2 tablespoons of the olive oil to a large pot over a medium-high heat. Once warm, add the sausage chunks and fry for about 8 minutes until nicely browned all over, stirring every so often. Remove from the pot and set aside on a plate. The sausages will have released a bit of fat, which is perfect for cooking the veg in.

Add a further 1–2 tablespoons of olive oil to the pot, depending on how much fat the sausages released, then add the leeks, celery and a pinch of salt and pepper. Fry over a medium heat for about 10 minutes until softened.

Add the potatoes and garlic and fry gently for 5 minutes, stirring every now and then. Add the tomato purée and fry for 2–3 minutes, stirring regularly, until it turns a darker shade of red.

Add the stock, beans and mustard and return the sausage chunks to the pot. Pop a lid on and simmer for 15 minutes until the veg is tender and the sausages are cooked through.

Just before serving, add the greens and cook for 3–5 minutes until wilted and tender. Taste for seasoning and ladle into bowls, sprinkling with chilli flakes if you like.

Tomato black bean broth

Feeds 2

Takes 15 minutes

2 tbsp olive oil

350g cherry tomatoes

1 bunch of spring onions,
   finely chopped

1 tsp cumin seeds

1 tsp coriander seeds

1 x 400g tin of black beans, drained
   and rinsed

500ml vegetable or chicken stock

1 lime

Sea salt and black pepper

FOR TOPPING

1 avocado, sliced

1 handful of fresh coriander leaves

Quick-pickled red onions (see page
   80, optional)

Mexican-inspired, with all the flavours of a great taco (you could even top this soup with tortilla chips for extra taco vibes). It's so quick and easy, and really fresh with the lime and coriander. If you can make a batch of quick-pickled red onions, they keep well in the fridge for up to a week and are a great addition here.

———————

Set a large pan over a high heat, add the olive oil and, once hot, add the cherry tomatoes. Cook for 3 minutes until blistered and charred, only stirring after a couple of minutes to give the tomatoes a chance to char slightly first. Scoop the tomatoes out of the pan and set aside on a plate.

Turn down the heat to medium, add the spring onions and season with salt and pepper. Fry for a couple of minutes until just beginning to soften, then add the cumin and coriander seeds and fry for a minute until fragrant. Add the black beans and pour in the stock, bring to the boil, then reduce the heat and simmer for 5–10 minutes while you prepare the toppings.

Squeeze the juice of half the lime into the broth, taste for seasoning, adding a little more lime juice if you like. Ladle into bowls and top with the avocado, coriander and quick-pickled red onions, if using.

One-pot lasagne
aka lazy lasagne

Feeds 4
Takes 1 hour, plus 15 minutes
resting

4 tbsp olive oil
400g beef mince
2 onions, finely chopped
2 carrots, finely chopped
4 big garlic cloves, finely chopped
2 tsp dried oregano, rosemary or
  mixed Italian herbs
4 tbsp tomato purée
1 x 400g tin of chopped tomatoes
1 x 400g tin of Puy or brown lentils,
  drained and rinsed
1 litre vegetable or meat stock
10 dried lasagne sheets
250g mozzarella or 125g mozzarella
  and 125g Cheddar or Parmesan,
  grated
Sea salt and black pepper

This is a lazy, untraditional take on lasagne made in one pot. There's no traditional white sauce as this means an extra step and an extra pot, instead you get a golden cheesy top layer, which is my favourite part anyway. The combination of mince and lentils means your mince goes further and you get the powered-up pulse factor from the lentils. I love eating this with a rocket salad, simply dressed with lemon juice and olive oil.

———————

Heat 2 tablespoons of the olive oil in a large, wide ovenproof pan and, once hot, add the mince and season. Cook over a medium-high heat for 8–10 minutes, breaking up the meat until nicely browned, then transfer to a bowl.

Preheat the oven to fan 190°C/gas mark 6½. Return the pan to the heat, add the remaining olive oil, then the onions, carrots and seasoning. Fry for 12 minutes until soft, stirring occasionally.

Next, add the garlic and most of the dried herbs (save some for topping) and fry for 2 minutes. Add the tomato purée and fry, stirring fairly continuously, for about 3 minutes until brick red. Return the mince to the pan.

Add the tinned tomatoes, lentils and stock. Stir well and simmer over a high heat, uncovered, for 5 minutes.

Break the lasagne sheets into large pieces, then add to the pan and push down using your wooden spoon so that they're covered in liquid. It will feel very liquidy but you need this liquid to cook the lasagne. Cover with a lid and transfer to the oven to cook for 25 minutes until the pasta is al dente (use a knife to test a piece of lasagne).

Remove from the oven and take off the lid. Tear over the mozzarella and season with salt and pepper and the reserved dried herbs. Turn the oven on to grill, at its highest heat, and grill for 5 minutes or until golden and bubbling. Leave to rest for 15 minutes, then dig in.

One-pot

Throw-it-all-in lentils
and garlic lime yoghurt

Feeds 4
Takes 25 minutes

1 x 400ml tin of full-fat coconut milk
700ml vegetable or chicken stock
400g cherry tomatoes
250g split red lentils, rinsed
2 tbsp medium curry powder
Small thumb of fresh ginger, finely
  grated
4 big garlic cloves, finely grated
250g frozen spinach
2 handfuls of frozen peas
Sea salt and black pepper

FOR THE GARLIC LIME YOGHURT
1 tbsp cumin seeds
200g yoghurt
Zest and juice of 1 lime
1 small garlic clove, finely grated

Inspired by a dahl, this is one for nights when you have no energy to watch over the hob and want a comforting bowl in 25 minutes flat. I like to dollop the garlic lime yoghurt on roasted veg and use it to dip flatbreads in too (see page 202). Frozen spinach is a game changer and really helps me make sure I get some green in my dinners even when the fridge is empty.

———————————

Start by toasting the cumin seeds for the garlic lime yoghurt in a dry pot (a large pot as you'll be using this for the lentils straight after) over a medium heat for a few minutes until they begin to pop. Tip into a small bowl.

Return the pot to a medium-high heat and throw in all the ingredients for the lentils, except the spinach and peas. Season with a good pinch of salt and pepper. Bring to the boil, then reduce to a simmer, cover and cook for 15 minutes until the lentils are very nearly tender. Stir every now and then to make sure the lentils don't catch on the bottom of the pot.

Stir in the spinach and peas and cook, uncovered, for 3–5 minutes until the spinach has wilted (timings will depend on whether the spinach is frozen in blocks or not).

Meanwhile, make the garlic lime yoghurt by adding the yoghurt, lime zest and juice and garlic to the bowl of toasted cumin seeds along with a pinch of sea salt.

Taste the lentils for seasoning, then serve up each bowl topped with the garlic lime yoghurt.

Puttanesca bean gratin

Feeds 4

Takes 1 hour 10 minutes (lots of hands-off time)

5 tbsp olive oil

1 large onion, finely chopped

4 garlic cloves, finely sliced

2 large handfuls of pitted black olives (about 100g)

3 tbsp capers

8–10 anchovies, to taste

1 tsp chilli flakes

2 x 400g tins of white beans, drained and rinsed, or 1 x 660g jar white beans, drained (butter beans, cannellini beans or a mix)

2 x 400g tins of chopped tomatoes

250g mozzarella

Sea salt and black pepper

Inspired by puttanesca pasta sauce but powered up with beans in place of pasta. I adore the bubbling hot, golden, cheesy topping, but if you're dairy free or in a rush, you could skip it and enjoy this simply as a hearty bowl. Serve with a big green salad.

———————

Heat 4 tablespoons of the olive oil in a shallow, ovenproof pot and, once warm, add the onion and a pinch of salt and pepper. Fry over a medium heat for about 10 minutes until soft, then add the garlic and fry for a couple of minutes. Add the olives, capers, anchovies and chilli flakes. Fry for a minute or two until the anchovies dissolve into the oil.

Add the beans and the chopped tomatoes. Swill out the tomato tins with a splash of water (about a quarter of the way up each tin) and add this too. Bring to a simmer and then cook for 30–35 minutes, stirring every so often to ensure it doesn't stick to the bottom of the pot, until thick and reduced.

Preheat the oven to fan 220°C/gas mark 9. Once the beans are reduced and thick, taste for seasoning. If your pot isn't ovenproof, transfer the beans to a baking dish at this stage. Tear over the mozzarella, season the mozzarella with salt and pepper and drizzle over the remaining tablespoon of olive oil. Transfer to the oven and bake for 20 minutes until the mozzarella is golden and bubbling. If you want to get a little more colour on the mozzarella, you can always switch to the grill setting for a few minutes at the end.

Mighty Monday minestrone

Feeds 6
Takes 40 minutes

4 tbsp olive oil, plus extra
  for drizzling
1 large onion, finely chopped
3 celery sticks, finely chopped
3 carrots, finely chopped
3 garlic cloves, finely chopped
1 tsp dried oregano or thyme
Pinch of chilli flakes
1 large jar of passata (about 700g)
1.5 litres vegetable or chicken stock
2 x 400g tins of beans, drained
  and rinsed
200g dried small pasta
200g leafy greens, sliced
Sea salt and black pepper

Minestrone is a forever favourite, all day any day, but I often end up making it on a Monday evening as it's a great way to start the week off right with lots of veg, and it means plenty of leftovers too, which feels like one less thing on the week's To Do list. You could also take a flask of it to work for lunch. It's 'mighty' as it's superpowered with beans and six different veg too. If you can find them, borlotti beans are great here and pasta shape wise, little pasta works well or roughly break up some dried spaghetti – you want to be able to eat this with a spoon!

—————————

Heat the olive oil in a large pot, then add the onion, celery and carrots with a pinch of salt and pepper and fry over a medium heat for 12–15 minutes until soft and lightly golden. Add the garlic, fry for a minute until fragrant, then add the oregano or thyme and chilli flakes and fry for another minute.

Add the passata and simmer for 10 minutes until reduced and thick. Add the stock and beans, bring to the boil, then add the pasta and cook for 8 minutes (or according to the packet instructions), adding the greens for the last couple of minutes. I like my minestrone thick and hearty, but if you'd like to add a little more stock, go for it. Taste for seasoning, then serve up each bowl with a good drizzle of olive oil.

One-pot

Filipino lemongrass coconut chicken

Feeds 4

Takes 45 minutes

4 bone-in, skin-on chicken thighs
3 tbsp olive oil or coconut oil
1 large brown onion, diced
Thumb of fresh ginger, finely
  chopped
4 garlic cloves, finely chopped
1/4 tsp ground turmeric
Pinch of chilli flakes
1 lemongrass stalk, outer stalks
  discarded, then roughly smashed
  with the side of a chef's knife
300g new potatoes (about 12),
  halved or quartered if large,
  or equivalent weight of large
  potatoes, chopped into
  bite-sized chunks
1 x 400ml tin of full-fat coconut milk
200g baby spinach
Sea salt and black pepper
White rice, to serve (optional)

A one-pot recipe but I'm cheating slightly as I'd like to recommend you enjoy this with a bowl of steaming hot rice to share. This is a fusion of a few of my favourite Filipino childhood meals. My mum tells me that in her hometown in the Philippines they'd use green (unripe) papaya and chilli leaves, but in MY hometown in the London suburbs, she'd swap them for potato and spinach as she couldn't find the ingredients easily in the 80s and 90s. This would be delicious with cubes of fish or chicken breast too and would cook much quicker.

———————

Season the chicken thighs on both sides. Heat half the oil in a large pot, add the chicken thighs, skin-side down, and fry over a medium-high heat for 10–12 minutes until well browned. Turn the chicken thighs and fry for another 5 minutes. Remove from the pot and set aside on a plate.

Add the remaining oil to the pot, then the onion, ginger, garlic, turmeric, chilli flakes and lemongrass, and season with salt and pepper. Turn down the heat and fry for 7–8 minutes until soft, stirring every now and then. Add the potatoes, coconut milk and chicken thighs, skin-side up. Cover and cook over a medium heat for 20–25 minutes until the potatoes are tender.

If serving with rice, rinse the rice and cook in a separate pot, according to the packet instructions.

Remove and discard the lemongrass. Add the spinach to the pot and let it wilt. Then take off the heat and adjust the seasoning with salt and pepper. Serve with the hot white rice, if you like.

Shepherd's pie with layered potatoes

Feeds 4
Takes 1 hour 20 minutes, plus
10 minutes resting (plenty of
hands-off time)

4 tbsp olive oil
400g mince, such as beef, lamb,
 chicken or turkey
2 onions, finely chopped
2 celery sticks, diced
3 carrots, diced, or a mix of
 prepped and diced squash,
 parsnip and swede
3 garlic cloves, finely chopped
1 tbsp dried mixed herbs (oregano,
 thyme or herbes de Provence)
1 tbsp flour (plain, gluten-free or
 chickpea flour)
3 tbsp tomato purée
1 x 400g tin of green or brown
 lentils, drained and rinsed
700ml vegetable or chicken stock
Sea salt and black pepper

FOR THE TOPPING
500g potatoes, finely sliced
2 tbsp olive oil

This dish is a hearty one-pot with both mince and lentils. I think everyone loves shepherd's pie, even little picky eaters, and this one is weeknight friendly – there's no need to make mash and dirty another pot, just top with thinly sliced potatoes that have been tossed in olive oil, salt and pepper. You'll be fighting over the crispy top. I never peel potatoes, just scrub them and save even more time! Use beef, lamb, chicken or turkey mince. Delicious with a simple green salad or a bowl of buttered peas.

———————

Heat 2 tablespoons of the olive oil in a large, ovenproof pan. Add the mince and season. Fry for 8–10 minutes over a medium-high heat, breaking up the mince, until browned. Scoop out of the pan (if using lamb, there may be some excess rendered fat, leave it in the pan for extra flavour).

Add the remaining olive oil to the pan with the onions, celery and carrots. Season and fry for about 8 minutes until soft. Add the garlic and dried herbs and fry for 1–2 minutes.

Return the mince to the pot, then sprinkle in the flour. Cook out the flour for 2 minutes, stirring regularly. Add the tomato purée and cook for a few minutes, stirring constantly, until a darker shade of red. Then add the lentils and stock, using your wooden spoon to scrape up any sticky bits from the bottom of the pan. Simmer for about 25 minutes until the sauce has reduced and thickened. Season with salt and pepper to taste. If the sauce looks a little dry, add another splash of stock or water.

Meanwhile, preheat the oven to fan 220°C/gas mark 9. Toss the potato slices with the olive oil, salt and pepper. Top the mince base with the potatoes, arranging them in a pretty pattern if you like or just freestyle it! Bake for 30 minutes until the mince base is bubbling and the potatoes are golden and tender. Leave to rest for 10–15 minutes so that the mixture can settle, making it easier to serve.

One-pot

Harira-style soup

Feeds 4
Takes 40 minutes

3 tbsp olive oil
1 large onion, finely chopped
2 celery sticks, finely chopped
2 large carrots, chopped into
  bite-sized pieces
4 garlic cloves, finely sliced
1 tbsp ground cumin
1 tbsp smoked paprika
1 tsp ground turmeric
1 tsp ground cinnamon
2 tbsp tomato purée
2 x 400g tins of green lentils,
  drained and rinsed
1 x 400g tin of chickpeas, drained
  and rinsed
1 litre vegetable or chicken stock
Zest and juice of 1 lemon
Sea salt and black pepper

TO SERVE
Yoghurt
Aleppo/urfa chilli flakes or regular
  chilli flakes

The Moroccan classic harira is the inspiration for this amazing soup, which is loaded up with trusty storecupboard favourites like lentils and chickpeas, plus warming spices. If you want to keep this plant-based, use veg stock and finish with coconut yoghurt or kefir on top.

———————

Heat the olive oil in a large pot. Add the onion, celery, carrots and a pinch of salt and pepper and fry over a medium heat for 12–15 minutes until soft.

Add the garlic and spices and fry for a couple of minutes until fragrant. Stir in the tomato purée and fry for 2–3 minutes until it turns brick red.

Add the lentils, chickpeas and stock. Cover with a lid and simmer for 15 minutes, stirring halfway through.

Add the lemon zest and juice. Taste for seasoning, then ladle into bowls and top with yoghurt and chilli flakes.

One-pot

Stock

Often stock cubes have an especially long list of ingredients that we might want to eat less of. Making your own stock sounds like a faff but it's easy enough and, if you have freezer space, it's great to store some there for a future gravy or soup base. I also love that homemade stock means that you can use up odds and ends of veg – it's great to get free flavour out of things we might normally throw away or waste.

Vegetable stock

4 garlic cloves, roughly chopped
Onion, leek, carrot or celery ends
1 handful of fresh herb stems
1 small handful of fresh thyme or
  1 tbsp dried mixed herbs
2 bay leaves
1 tsp black peppercorns or
  ½ tsp black pepper
Parmesan rind (optional)
2–3 litres water

Add all the ingredients to a large pan or slow cooker. Cover with a lid, bring to the boil, then reduce to a low simmer and cook for at least 1 hour.

Strain and leave to cool before storing in the fridge for 4–5 days or in the freezer for up to 3 months.

Meat stock

1–3kg uncooked or cooked bones
  or chicken carcasses
2–3 litres water
1 tbsp apple cider vinegar
Onion, leek, carrot or celery ends
1 handful of fresh herb stems
2 bay leaves
1 tsp black peppercorns or
  ½ tsp black pepper

Add all the ingredients to a large pan or slow cooker. Cover with a lid, bring to the boil, then reduce to a low simmer for 2–3 hours, or up to 6 hours if using a slow cooker.

Strain and leave to cool before storing in the fridge for 4–5 days or in the freezer for up to 3 months.

HOW
TO
BUILD
A...
soup

Stock, broth or water?

Chicken or vegetable stock, water with miso paste – it goes without saying that the more flavour you have in the liquid you're adding, the more flavour you'll have in the final soup. See page 153 for homemade stock recipes.

Veggies

Root veggies like squash, parsnips, potatoes or sweet potatoes. Be flexible on things like greens, swapping kale for cabbage, spinach or Swiss chard, for example.

Base

Choose oil or butter and a few from: onions, leeks, spring onions, garlic, fresh ginger, chillies, whole or ground spices.

One-pot

Make it hearty

Add pasta, noodles, a handful or two of cooked chickpeas, beans or lentils.

**To blend
or not to blend?**
You decide!

Toppings

Crunchy
Toasted seeds and nuts, crispy chickpeas, crispy grains or fried halloumi croutons.

Swirly
Crème fraîche, yoghurt, a little miso or harissa paste, chilli oil, pestos, herby drizzles, salsas or just a lovely splash of a good olive oil.

Fresh
Chopped fresh herbs, a squeeze of lemon or lime juice to brighten.

Finish

Fried
Fry some spices in olive oil to drizzle over the top, or fry some sliced garlic or shallots to add flavour and crunch at the end.

Fermented
Add a little dollop of probiotic-rich kimchi, sauerkraut or kefir.

Cheesy
Grated hard cheese like Cheddar or Parmesan or crumbled feta or goat's cheese.

Batch cooking

Chatting about batch cooking with friends and on social media, people seem to split into fans who swear by it for an easier life, and those who feel that batch cooking is a false economy or think it means eating the same boring leftovers for four days straight.

For me, batch cooking is a saviour during weeks when you have a full schedule or lots of people visiting. I find it reassuring to know that there are containers of something delicious in the freezer (like the **Harissa Lentil Pie with Feta Mash** on page 164), for those days when you might otherwise find yourself turning to a convenient ready meal or expensive takeaway. As well as saving on time and your own energy, it can also help with food waste as you're defrosting only what you need, when you need it.

For those of you that have limited freezer space, you don't have to go big on batch cooking. It can be as simple as 'cook once, eat twice', by simply doubling up on dinner to leave yourself leftovers in the fridge to roll into tomorrow's lunchbox or supper.

There are also ways to make up a big batch of a base recipe which can be flexed so you don't end up eating the same thing multiple nights in a row. See the **3 Ways with...** on pages 20–1 for different ways to use the **Red Lentil and Tomato Super Sauce** on page 160, plus further inspiration to make the most of a big batch cook.

If you're a batch cooking convert, there are some other recipes in the book which double up really well, for example the **Peperonata Pasta sauce** on page 86, or **Lemony Lentil Carrot Soup** on page 132.

Red lentil and tomato super sauce

Makes 12 portions
Takes 1 hour (only 20 minutes hands-on time)

8 tbsp olive oil
3 onions, finely chopped
6 garlic cloves, finely chopped
Pinch of chilli flakes (optional)
3 tbsp tomato purée
200g split red lentils, rinsed
3 x 400g tins of chopped tomatoes
Sea salt and black pepper

This is a tasty multipurpose tomato sauce with hidden nutritious red lentils. Blend it into a smooth, protein-packed tomato sauce for spaghetti or your favourite pasta, or loosen it up a little by adding veggie stock to turn it into a creamy (but cream-less) soup, lovely with a cheese toastie.

Enjoy the flexibility of the sauce by serving it in different ways, see page 20.

———————

Heat the olive oil in a large pot and, once warm, add the onions, then season with salt and pepper. Fry for 12–15 minutes over a medium heat until golden and soft. Add the garlic and chilli flakes, then fry for a couple of minutes until fragrant. Add the tomato purée and fry for 2–3 minutes until brick red.

Add the lentils and tinned tomatoes. Fill two of the three empty tomato tins with water and use the water to swill out all the last bits of tomato. Add this water to the pot and season with salt and pepper.

Bring up to the boil, then reduce the heat to a simmer and cook for 30–35 minutes, uncovered, stirring occasionally so that it doesn't stick to the bottom of the pot, until the lentils have completely broken down. Add another half tomato tin of water if you need more liquid.

Using a stick blender or a blender, blitz the sauce until smooth or, if you prefer some texture in your sauce, blitz roughly half and leave the rest chunky. Season to taste.

Batch cooking

Root veg and onion crumble

Feeds 4
Takes 1 hour 45 minutes
(25 minutes hands-on time),
plus 20 minutes resting

750g root veg, such as potatoes,
  celeriac, squash and/or parsnips,
  cut into 3mm-thick slices
50g unsalted butter
4 large onions (about 700g),
  finely sliced
100g kale or cavolo nero, roughly
  torn or shredded
250ml vegetable or chicken stock
1 heaped tbsp Dijon mustard
75g Cheddar, coarsely grated
¼ nutmeg kernel, finely grated
Sea salt and black pepper

FOR THE CRUMBLE TOPPING
100g rolled oats
100g cold unsalted butter, cubed
100g whole hazelnuts, roughly
  chopped
100g Cheddar, coarsely grated
Pinch of chilli flakes (optional)
Drizzle of olive oil, for topping

One of my most popular dishes since I started sharing recipes is a vegetable crumble. So, here's my new favourite way to enjoy it. This makes a fantastic veg main for a Sunday roast dinner or make it on a Monday evening using leftover vegetables from the week before. Once your bubbling golden crumble is out of the oven, let it rest for at least 20 minutes so that the stock can be further absorbed into the root veg. Serve with a crunchy green salad and extra Dijon mustard.

———————

Preheat the oven to fan 180°C/gas mark 6. Spread the sliced root veg out in a large, deep baking dish (about 30 x 20cm) and season with salt and pepper.

Heat the butter in a large saucepan and, once foaming, add the onions and a good pinch of salt. Cover and fry over a medium heat for 15 minutes, then remove the lid and continue to fry, stirring every so often, for another 10 minutes until very soft. If the onions start to catch, reduce the heat and add a little splash of water.

In a large jug, whisk together the stock, Dijon mustard, cheese and nutmeg. Season with salt and pepper, then pour over the root veg in the dish. Top with the softened onions and kale.

For the crumble topping, rub together the oats and butter with a pinch of salt and pepper until it resembles a crumble mixture. Mix in the hazelnuts, Cheddar and chilli flakes, if using. Scatter over the veg, then bake for 50 minutes–1 hour until the top is golden and the veg is completely tender (check by inserting a knife, it should go through the veg with very little resistance). Leave to rest for 20–30 minutes before serving (don't skip this step: it allows the stock to absorb further into the root veg; if you dive in straight away it will be too liquidy).

Batch cooking

Harissa lentil pie
with feta mash

Feeds 6
Takes 1 hour 35 minutes (plenty of hands-off time)

4 tbsp olive oil
2 onions, finely chopped
2 carrots, finely chopped
2 celery sticks, finely chopped
2 peppers (any colour), finely chopped
4 garlic cloves, finely chopped
3 tbsp tomato purée
4–5 tbsp harissa paste, to taste
200g brown lentils, rinsed
750ml vegetable or chicken stock
250g frozen spinach
Sea salt and black pepper

FOR THE MASH
1kg potatoes (peeled if you prefer), chopped into large chunks
80g unsalted butter
200g feta

Packed with vegetables and lentils, this is a big, beautiful pie. It's my kind of Sunday night supper, with leftovers to roll over into the following night. Mashed potatoes are delicious in their simplicity but add some feta and you're at next-level mash magnificence. Adjust the harissa amounts depending on the strength of your harissa paste and how spicy you like things. Use fresh or frozen spinach and change up your pepper and onion colours for veg variety.

———————————

Put the potatoes for the mash in a large pot of salted water. Bring to the boil, then cook for 12–15 minutes until fork tender, then drain.

Meanwhile, heat the olive oil in a separate large pot and, once warm, add the onions, carrots, celery and peppers. Season with salt and pepper. Fry over a medium heat for 15–20 minutes until everything is very soft. Add the garlic and fry for a further minute or two until fragrant.

Add the tomato purée, then fry for 2–3 minutes until brick red. Add the harissa, lentils and stock. Bring to a simmer and cook for 20 minutes until the lentils are tender.

As the lentils cook, return to the mash. Return the drained potatoes to their pot, add the butter and mash to your preferred consistency. Crumble in the feta (I like to keep it quite chunky), stir to incorporate and season to taste.

Preheat the oven to fan 200°C/gas mark 7.

Once the lentils are tender, add the spinach and cook for a few minutes until just wilted. Season to taste, then transfer to a large baking dish and top with the feta mash. Bake for 30–35 minutes until golden and bubbling.

Storecupboard tomato butter beans with feta and dill

Feeds 6
Takes 50 minutes (only 20 minutes hands-on time)

4 tbsp extra virgin olive oil,
  plus extra to serve
3 onions, thinly sliced
4 garlic cloves, thinly sliced
1 tbsp cumin seeds
1 cinnamon stick, snapped in half
  or ¼ tsp ground cinnamon
Chilli flakes, to taste, plus extra
  (optional) to serve
1 handful of fresh oregano leaves
  or 2 tsp dried oregano
3 tbsp tomato purée
4 x 400g tins of chopped tomatoes
3 x 400g tins of butter beans,
  drained and rinsed
400g feta, thinly sliced or crumbled
Sea salt and black pepper
2 large handfuls of fresh dill or 2 tsp
  dried dill, to serve

Inspired by holidays in Greece, this is delicious straight from the pan, served warm or cold the next day mezze-style. All the ingredients are cupboard staples or everyday ingredients, so it's a dependable recipe to have up your sleeve. Check out the easy flatbreads recipe on page 202, which are the perfect accompaniment.

———————

Heat the olive oil in a large pot, then add the onions and a good pinch of salt and pepper. Fry over a medium heat for about 12 minutes until soft and golden. Add the garlic, spices and oregano. Fry for 2 minutes, stirring regularly, until fragrant. Add the tomato purée and fry for 2–3 minutes, stirring regularly, until brick red.

Add the tinned tomatoes (make sure to get every last bit of tomato flavour by swirling the empty tins with a little splash of water) and butter beans, bring to a simmer, then cook for 25–30 minutes, uncovered, until reduced and thick.

Top with the feta, dill, a drizzle of olive oil and extra chilli flakes, if you like.

Batch cooking

Spiced bean bake with cheesy potato mash and jalapeño drizzle

Serves 6
Takes 1 hour 15 minutes

FOR THE BEAN BASE
2 tbsp olive oil
2 onions, finely chopped
2 red or orange peppers, diced
3 large garlic cloves, finely
  chopped
1 tbsp dried oregano
1½ tsp ground cumin
1½ tsp ground coriander
Pinch of chilli flakes
½ tsp smoked paprika
2 tbsp tomato purée
2 x 400g tins of mixed beans,
  drained and rinsed
150g tinned or frozen sweetcorn
2 x 400g tins of chopped tomatoes
250ml vegetable or chicken stock
Sea salt and black pepper

FOR THE CHEESY MASH
1.2 kg potatoes (peeled if you
  prefer), roughly chopped
60g unsalted butter
150g mature Cheddar, grated

FOR THE DRIZZLE
6 spring onions, finely chopped
2 tbsp pickled green jalapeños,
  finely chopped
1 tbsp brine from the jalapeño jar
1 small bunch of fresh coriander,
  finely chopped
Juice of 2 limes
6 tbsp extra virgin olive oil

Who doesn't love cheesy mash? Keep things traditional with potato mash or change it up with a mixture of potato and parsnips or celeriac or squash too. Mash is a great way to increase your variety of veg and they all cook in roughly the same amount of time. If you're cooking for kids and think they might not fancy the delicious drizzle, just drizzle it over half the pie. It's so good, they might be tempted to try it.

Set a large, ovenproof pot – mine has a diameter of 23cm – over a medium heat and add the olive oil. Once warm, add the onions and some salt and pepper and fry for 10 minutes until soft. Add the diced peppers and fry for another 5 minutes.

Add the garlic, oregano and spices and fry for a couple of minutes until fragrant. Add the tomato purée and fry for 2–3 minutes until brick red. Add the beans, sweetcorn (drained if tinned), chopped tomatoes and stock. Simmer for 20 minutes.

Meanwhile, bring a large pan of salted water to the boil for the mash. Cook the potatoes (and parsnips if using) in the salted water for 15 minutes until fork tender. Drain and mash with the butter. Season to taste with salt and pepper.

As the potatoes cook, preheat the oven to fan 200°C/gas mark 7.

Once the bean base has finished simmering, check for seasoning, then top with the mash and scatter over the grated Cheddar. Bake in the oven for 20–25 minutes until golden and bubbling.

Leave the pie to rest for 10 minutes while you make the jalapeño drizzle. Mix all the ingredients together in a small bowl and season to taste. Serve the pie with the drizzle spooned over it.

Big batch, lots of veg bolognese

Makes about 10 portions
Takes 5 hours (1 hour
hands-on time)

6 tbsp olive oil
800g beef mince
2 large onions
2 celery sticks
2 large carrots
1 fennel bulb
1 courgette
1 leek
250g mushrooms
3 garlic cloves
2 bay leaves
1 small handful of woody herbs,
  such as thyme, sage or rosemary,
  leaves picked
2 tbsp tomato purée
2 x 400g tins of chopped tomatoes
150ml milk
Sea salt and black pepper

I counted eight different types of veg in this bolognese. Yes, it's a time-consuming big batch (I actually often double this to make 20 portions, you'll need two pans on the go if you want to do this), but I love knowing that my favourite comfort food is ready to go in the freezer for a busy week. You could use a food processor to speed up the veg prep if you have one, or pop on a good podcast or playlist and get in the chopping zone! If you can bear it, this is even better the next day, so try to make it at least a day before you want to eat it, but I find it impossible to smell it simmering all afternoon and then not eat it. Serve with your favourite pasta (I like rigatoni for this), use for lasagne (see page 142), or pile it on toast, top with cheese and grill. If you have Parmesan rinds, throw them in when everything is bubbling away beautifully.

———————

Get your largest pot over a medium-high heat and add 3 tablespoons of the olive oil. Once shimmering, add the mince and season with salt and pepper. Cook for 10–15 minutes, breaking up the meat until nicely browned.

As the mince browns, finely chop all the veg and the garlic.

Once the meat is browned, transfer to a large bowl and set aside. Return the pot to the heat and add the remaining 3 tablespoons of olive oil. Once shimmering, add all the veg, except the mushrooms. Season with salt and pepper and cook over a medium heat for 15 minutes until softened. Then add the mushrooms, garlic and herbs and cook for another 10 minutes until the mushroom liquid has evaporated. Add the tomato purée and cook for another few minutes until it turns a darker shade of red.

Add the mince back to the pot along with the tinned tomatoes and milk. Simmer for 3–4 hours, stirring every now and then to ensure it's not sticking on the bottom of the pot. Check the seasoning and serve with your favourite pasta and some grated Parmesan if you like.

Batch cooking

Soothing kitchari-style rice and lentils

Feeds 4
Takes 30 minutes

100g white basmati rice
300g split red lentils
2 litres vegetable or chicken stock
2 tsp cumin seeds
1 tsp fennel seeds
2 tsp black mustard seeds
3 tbsp ghee or coconut oil
1 large onion, finely chopped
2 garlic cloves, finely chopped
Large thumb of fresh ginger, finely chopped or grated
2 tsp ground turmeric
1 tsp chilli powder or chilli flakes, to taste
200g greens like chard, leaves and stems roughly chopped
Sea salt

My friend, the chef Romy Gill, made me her famous kitchari one day when she came over, and when she left, I couldn't stop thinking about it. Kitchari, also known as kitchadi, is perfect for when we could all do with a bit of comfort and soothing from a warm bowl of spiced rice and lentils. I turn to it when I'm feeling a bit under the weather too.

———————

Wash the rice and lentils together several times under cold water until the water runs clear. This is an essential step! Pop them into a big pan, pour over the stock, stir well, pop a lid on and simmer for 20 minutes, stirring every now and then, especially at the bottom of the pan to make sure the lentils don't stick. Add more stock or water if needed.

Meanwhile, in a large frying pan, toast the cumin, fennel and black mustard seeds over a medium heat for a few minutes until fragrant. Then add the ghee or coconut oil, onion, garlic, ginger, turmeric, chilli powder or flakes and a pinch of salt and fry gently over a low heat for about 10–12 minutes, stirring occasionally.

When the rice and lentils are softened, spoon all the onion mixture in but keep the frying pan you used for the onions – you're going to fry the greens in the leftover flavoured oil. Stir the rice, lentils and onion mixture together and season to taste.

Return the frying pan to a medium heat and add the greens. Fry for 3–5 minutes until wilted and tender. Serve the kitchari in bowls with the greens on top.

Moroccan lamb meatballs

Feeds 6

Takes 50 minutes

800g lamb mince

1 red onion, finely chopped

2 garlic cloves, finely chopped

2 tbsp ras el hanout or harissa
   paste

3 handfuls of fresh mint leaves,
   finely chopped

100g dried apricots, finely chopped

100g thick yoghurt, plus extra
   to serve

3 tbsp olive oil

Sea salt and black pepper

FOR THE SAUCE

3 tbsp olive oil

2 red onions, finely chopped

2 garlic cloves, finely chopped

Pinch of chilli flakes

3 x 400g tins of chopped tomatoes

These meatballs are great to make with kids, as their little hands are perfect for rolling the mixture. Leftovers will freeze nicely. I love to serve them with yoghurt, fresh mint leaves and flatbreads or pitta – give the easy peasy flatbreads recipe on page 202 a go. Also delicious served with quinoa, rice or couscous.

―――――――――

First, get the sauce on. Heat the olive oil in a large pot and, once warm, add the onions and season with salt and pepper. Fry for 10–12 minutes over a medium heat, stirring occasionally, until soft. Add the garlic and chilli flakes, then cook for a minute or two, stirring continuously, until fragrant. Add the tinned tomatoes and fill up one of the tins with water to swill out all the last bits of tomatoes in the tins. Bring to the boil, then reduce to a gentle simmer and cook for 25–30 minutes as you make the meatballs. Stir every so often to ensure nothing sticks to the bottom of the pot.

As the sauce simmers, preheat the oven to fan 180°C/ gas mark 6. In a large mixing bowl, mix all the meatball ingredients, except the olive oil, with some salt and pepper. Hands are the best tool here to ensure that everything is evenly distributed. Roll into 24 balls, roughly the size of a golf ball, and place on a large roasting tray. Drizzle with the olive oil and bake for 25–30 minutes until nicely browned and cooked through.

Gently stir the meatballs through the sauce or keep the two separate if you prefer. Serve with extra yoghurt.

One for now, one for later banana bread

Makes 2 loaves

Takes 1 hour 20 minutes
(most is hands-off time)

60g unsalted butter or coconut oil

8 very ripe bananas

4 tbsp maple syrup

2 tsp ground cinnamon

2 tsp vanilla extract

6 eggs

2 tsp bicarbonate of soda

Juice of 1 lemon

200g ground almonds

200g spelt or plain flour (or another
   200g ground almonds to make
   this gluten-free)

3 handfuls of chopped nuts, such
   as pecans or hazelnuts

3 handfuls of raisins, chopped
   dried fruit or chocolate chunks

Sea salt

Freestyle the fruit and nuts here – my fave current combination is pecans and raisins. This banana bread will keep in a sealed container at room temperature for 2 days. If putting one of the loaves in the freezer, allow it to cool completely, then slice and freeze in airtight pouches or freezer bags. Bake from frozen in a fan 180°C/gas mark 6 oven until defrosted all the way through and lightly toasted. Or defrost on the kitchen counter first, then pop in the toaster.

———————

Preheat the oven to fan 170°C/gas mark 5 and line two loaf tins with baking parchment (I use this paper after baking to wrap the bread in). Melt the butter or coconut oil in a saucepan and allow it to cool slightly.

In a large mixing bowl, mash six of the bananas to a pulp with a fork. Slice the remaining bananas (either lengthways or into coins) and set aside for decoration. Add the maple syrup, melted butter, cinnamon, vanilla, eggs, bicarbonate of soda, lemon juice and a good pinch of salt. Mix well. Add the ground almonds, flour, nuts and dried fruit or chocolate chunks and mix well.

Pour the batter into the lined tins and top with the banana halves or coins, pushing them in a bit. Bake for about 50 minutes, keeping an eye on them for the last 5 minutes or so for browning on the top (insert a skewer in the middle, which will come out clean when they're baked). Allow to cool in the tins for 15 minutes before removing.

Batch cooking

Sweets

I adore a sweet treat as much as the next person but, like Snacks (see pages 197–217), they can be one of the easiest places to fall into a UPF trap. Whether it's overly-processed ice cream, long-life cakes or pastries, or just the 4pm chocolate bar – a lot of our favourite sweet snacks have been designed to have as long a shelf-life as possible, which as we know usually means they are high in UPFs.

In this chapter, I've tried to give some alternatives so that we can still enjoy all the treats we love but without those additives or the dreaded sugar crash. Whether it's something for the 4pm slump (**Chocolate Date Tahini Bites** on page 185), a treat for after school pick-ups (**Double Apple and Cinnamon Oat Bars** on page 187) or something to satisfy the post-dinner sweet craving (**Five-minute Berry Fro-Yo** on page 188), I hope you'll find something to satisfy your sweet tooth on every occasion.

For when a craving hits and you only have two minutes, you can't beat a fruit dipper (page 216) whether it's chocolate-covered or dipped into a nut butter. If all else fails, a handful of granola (page 32) is amazing.

When you're shopping, look out for Fairtrade certified products when you can, especially for ingredients like chocolate, vanilla, tea and coffee. I've been an ambassador for Fairtrade for ten years and seen firsthand the difference that fair pay makes to farmers, their families and their communities around the world.

Carrot cake oat cookies

Makes 20
Takes 50 minutes
Keeps for 3 days, at room
temperature

250g rolled oats
1 tsp baking powder
2 tsp ground cinnamon
¼ nutmeg, finely grated
Little pinch of sea salt
2 small carrots, coarsely grated
Zest of 1 orange
50g raisins
50g walnuts or pecans,
* roughly chopped*
80g unsalted butter
4 tbsp maple syrup

All the classic flavours of carrot cake, in cookie format.
With oats as their base, a hit of veg from the carrot and
a good dose of walnuts, I've happily grabbed some of
these cookies for a makeshift breakfast on the run when
I've been rushing for an early morning meeting.

———————

Preheat the oven to fan 170°C/gas mark 5. Line a large
baking tray, or two medium ones, with baking parchment.

Blitz half the oats in a food processor to the consistency of
flour. Add to a mixing bowl with the whole oats, the baking
powder, spices and salt. Stir well to combine.

Mix in the grated carrot, orange zest, raisins and walnuts or
pecans. In a small saucepan, melt the butter, then add to
the bowl with the maple syrup. Stir to evenly distribute.

Take a heaped tablespoon of the mixture at a time and roll
into 20 balls. Then flatten slightly to create thick cookies
and push any rogue raisins in so they don't burn. Place
on the lined baking tray(s) and bake for 30 minutes, or until
lightly set and golden. Allow to cool completely on the
baking tray(s) and they will firm up.

Chocolate peanut butter
(no-bake) bars

Makes 16
Takes 20 minutes, plus
setting time
Keeps for 1 week, at room
temperature

250g smooth peanut butter
100g ground almonds
100g porridge oats
6 tbsp maple syrup
1 tsp vanilla extract
Little pinch of sea salt

FOR THE CHOCOLATE LAYER
180g dark chocolate, roughly
* broken*
1 tbsp smooth peanut butter
Flaky sea salt, for sprinkling

OPTIONAL TOPPING
2 handfuls of toasted peanuts

A no-bake family favourite treat. Pretty irresistible but if you don't devour them over a few days, they will keep for a week in a sealed container. Store in the fridge in warmer months. If catering to any nut allergies, swap the ground almonds for more oats and switch the nut butter for pumpkin seed butter. If you have a preferred nut butter, try that – I love a cashew butter but keep it to the smooth variety for a silkier texture. Look out for 60% minimum cocoa solids for your chocolate.

———————

Line a small tin or dish (about 15 x 8cm or square equivalent) with greaseproof paper, making sure it comes up high enough on the sides so that you can lift the mixture out of the tin once it's set.

Mix the peanut butter, ground almonds, oats, maple syrup, vanilla and salt together in a bowl. Transfer to the lined tin, pressing down with the back of a spoon or spatula to make it even and compact.

For the chocolate layer, melt the chocolate in a bain-marie (a heatproof bowl set over a pan of very lightly simmering water, making sure the bottom of the bowl does not touch the water). Once melted, stir through the peanut butter and pour this evenly over the base. If topping with the whole peanuts, scatter these over the chocolate layer. Sprinkle over a little pinch of flaky sea salt.

Set in the fridge for 1 hour or until firm, then cut into 16 pieces to serve.

Apricot and almond bumbles

Makes 12
Takes 30 minutes
Keeps for 3 days, at room
temperature

175g dried apricots
250g ground almonds
½ tsp baking powder
25g unsalted butter, melted
1 tsp vanilla extract
1 egg, beaten
100g dark chocolate, broken
  into pieces
Flaky sea salt, for sprinkling

I love a bumble (a crumbly biscuit). If you're in a rush, you don't need to drizzle these with chocolate but they are especially good with this extra touch. When it's a hot chocolate kind of night, I don't do the chocolate drizzle and instead dunk straight into my mug of hot choccy. In warmer months, keep in the fridge to prevent the chocolate from melting.

———————

Preheat the oven to fan 170°C/gas mark 5. Line a baking tray with baking parchment.

Finely chop the apricots. Add to a mixing bowl with the ground almonds, baking powder and a little pinch of salt. Mix well, then add the melted butter, vanilla and egg. Mix well to combine.

Taking a heaped tablespoon of the mixture at a time, roll into 12 balls, then flatten slightly to create thick cookies. Place on the lined baking tray and bake for 20–25 minutes until lightly golden. Allow the bumbles to cool completely on the baking tray.

Melt the chocolate in a bain-marie (a small heatproof bowl set over a pan of barely simmering water, making sure the bottom of the bowl does not touch the water). Then drizzle the bumbles with chocolate and sprinkle with a little flaky salt. Leave to set before serving.

Chocolate date tahini bites

Makes 15
Takes 10 minutes, plus
setting time
Keeps for 5 days, in the fridge

12 Medjool dates
5 tbsp tahini or your fave smooth
  nut butter (stirred well in the
  jar first)
100g dark chocolate, broken
  into pieces
1 handful of pistachios,
  roughly chopped
Flaky sea salt

These smashed, chewy, choc drizzled dates have gone internet viral and for very good reason. They are utterly moreish, delicious and use just five ingredients. Medjool dates tend to be the softest, so they work best here as there's less squishing effort required! Whenever you're using tahini or nut butters, stir the jar well first so that you get yourself a good amount of both solids and oil in your spoon.

———————

Line a 15cm square or rectangular dish with baking parchment. Halve, pit, then squish the dates into the dish to make a thinnish layer that evenly covers the base. Drizzle with the tahini or nut butter, then spread it over the dates to cover.

In a bain-marie (a heatproof bowl set over a pan of barely simmering water, making sure the bottom of the bowl does not touch the water), melt the chocolate, then pour this over the tahini or nut butter, making sure it gets to every edge and corner. Sprinkle over the pistachios, then transfer to the fridge to set for 1–2 hours.

Once set, sprinkle over a little sea salt, then cut into small bites and enjoy.

Double apple and cinnamon oat bars

Makes 16
Takes 50 minutes (just 10 minutes hands-on time), plus setting time
Keeps for 5 days, in the fridge

200g unsalted butter
200g runny honey
75g dried apples, finely chopped
2 eating apples, cored and coarsely grated
300g porridge oats
30g sunflower seeds (optional)
1 tsp ground cinnamon
Pinch of sea salt

A great nut-free option for travelling and lunchboxes, especially if your kids' schools or your workplace is nut free. The chewy dried apple is my favourite part (look out for dried apple pieces that are as squidgy and soft as possible), and these snacks are packed with fresh apple too. You could swap the apple for other dried fruit at a pinch and the sunflower seeds can be replaced with pumpkin seeds.

———————

Preheat the oven to fan 170°C/gas mark 5 and line a 23cm square baking tin with greaseproof paper.

Melt the butter in a medium saucepan, then pour in the honey and stir to combine. Add the dried and grated apples, stir well and make sure all the ingredients are evenly distributed. Leave to sit as you mix together all the dry ingredients in a large mixing bowl.

Add the wet ingredients to the dry ingredients and mix well. You really want to mix properly here so that everything is coated. Transfer to the lined baking tin and press down very well to form an even layer. Bake for 30–35 minutes until golden. As soon as you remove the tin from the oven, use the flat base of a pan (or another suitable kitchen item with a flat base) to press down the oaty mixture evenly. This helps the mixture to compact, meaning your bars will hold their shape better once cut.

Leave to cool completely. Leave to set in the fridge overnight if you can bear it (this helps them firm up more), then cut into 16 squares.

Five-minute berry fro-yo

Feeds 6–8

Takes 5 minutes

300g frozen berries or frozen
  (pitted) cherries
150g thick yoghurt or your favourite
  plant-based option
2 tbsp honey or maple syrup
Little pinch of sea salt

Fro-yo is frozen yoghurt if you haven't come across this speedy treat yet. It's best enjoyed straight away as the texture will be at its best straight from the food processor and it firms up a lot in the freezer. Make sure to use a food processor here rather than a blender because a blender overmixes, meaning the mixture becomes too runny. My favourite toppings to shout out are tahini, chopped pistachios and/or flaked almonds.

———————————

Put all the ingredients in a food processor and blitz until just combined, scraping down the sides once or twice as needed. Be very careful not to overmix, otherwise it will turn runny. Serve immediately with any toppings that you like.

Lemon blueberry muffins

Makes 12
Takes 45 minutes
Keeps for 2 days, at room
temperature

50g unsalted butter
2 lemons: zest of both, juice of 1
200g ground almonds
1 tsp baking powder
Tiny pinch of sea salt
5 tbsp maple syrup
1 tsp vanilla extract
3 eggs
250g fresh blueberries

Packed with juicy blueberries and lemon zest for freshness. These are made with ground almonds instead of flour, so will hopefully please everyone, including gluten-free friends (just make sure to use gluten-free baking powder too). Store in an airtight container for up to 2 days.

———————

Preheat the oven to fan 170°C/gas mark 5 and line a 12-hole muffin tray with paper cases.

Melt the butter in a small saucepan, then grate in all the lemon zest and leave to cool for a few minutes (this is so it doesn't scramble the eggs when you combine them later).

Meanwhile, in a large bowl, mix the ground almonds, baking powder and salt.

Pour in the butter and lemon zest mixture, add the lemon juice, maple syrup and vanilla and mix together. In another small bowl, whisk the eggs, then add to the muffin mixture and stir to combine. Gently fold in the blueberries.

Divide the batter between the muffin cases so that each one is about three-quarters full. Bake for 30 minutes until just lightly golden on top and a skewer comes out clean when inserted into the middle. (If you poke into a blueberry it obviously won't come out clean! So, try to insert the skewer into the sponge.)

Leave to cool in the tray, then enjoy.

Flourless chocolate cake with whipped espresso cream

Makes 10 slices
Takes 50 minutes, plus
cooling time
Keeps for 3 days, in the fridge

180g dark chocolate, broken
  into pieces
180g unsalted butter, diced
120ml maple syrup
1 tsp vanilla extract
5 eggs, separated
¼ tsp sea salt
100g ground almonds
Chocolate shavings, for topping
  (optional)

FOR THE ESPRESSO CREAM
300ml double cream
1 double espresso or 3 tbsp very
  strong instant coffee, cooled
1 tbsp cocoa powder

This is perfect for celebrations big and small, from birthdays to a 'we made it to the end of a busy week' bake. The whipped espresso cream makes it extra special; if you'd rather leave out the coffee, you could flavour the cream with orange zest and scatter with pomegranate seeds instead or just leave it 'naked'.

———————————

Preheat the oven to fan 170°C/gas mark 5 and line a 20cm round cake tin with greaseproof paper.

Gently melt the chocolate and butter in a bain-marie (a heatproof bowl set over a pan of barely simmering water, making sure the bottom of the bowl does not touch the water). When it's melted, remove from the heat and allow to cool for a few minutes, then stir in the maple syrup, vanilla, egg yolks and sea salt. Stir through the ground almonds and set aside.

In a second clean and dry bowl, whisk the egg whites until fluffy. Gently stir one big spoonful of the whisked egg whites into the chocolate bowl, then gently fold through the rest.

Spoon the finished mixture into the lined cake tin and bake for 25–28 minutes until a skewer inserted into the middle of the cake comes out clean. Allow to cool completely in the tin on a wire rack.

For the espresso cream, whip the cream to soft peaks, then gently fold in the cooled espresso or instant coffee. Once the cake has completely cooled, top with the cream and dust over the cocoa powder. Don't be tempted to top with the cream while the cake is still slightly warm or it will melt! Finish with chocolate shavings if you like.

Raid-the-cupboards chocolate bark

Makes 1 tray of bark
Takes 15 minutes, plus
setting time
Keeps for 1 week, in the fridge

200g dark chocolate, roughly
 chopped
75g white or milk chocolate,
 roughly chopped
1 large handful of dried fruit
 (see intro)
2 large handfuls of toasted nuts
 (see intro), roughly chopped

The easiest sweet treat and super customisable too, depending on what you fancy and what you've got in the cupboard. Get creative with your toppings and flavourings, using this recipe as a base. Dried fruit that works well includes raisins, cranberries, chopped apricots or mango. Almonds, pecans or hazelnuts are delicious options for the toasted nuts.

———————

Line a flat baking tray with greaseproof paper.

Set up a bain-marie (a heatproof bowl set over a pan of barely simmering water, making sure the bottom of the bowl does not touch the water) and gently melt the dark chocolate. Pour the dark chocolate onto the lined tray and smooth out until 3mm thick.

Wash out the bowl, then repeat the melting process for the white or milk chocolate. Take extra care as white chocolate really doesn't like to be overheated! Once melted, use a small spoon to drizzle the white or milk chocolate over the dark chocolate base. Scatter over the dried fruit and nuts, then transfer to the fridge to set for at least 1 hour. Once set, break into shards and serve immediately or store in an airtight container in the fridge for up to a week.

Alternative flavour combinations/additions:

Grate orange zest into the dark chocolate base.
Drizzle with **tahini** and top with **mixed seeds**.
Hazelnuts and milk chocolate for you-know-what vibes.
Toasted **pecans** and dried **cranberries**.
Freeze-dried **raspberries** with **white chocolate**.
Peppermint extract for that chocolate mint feel.

Snacks

I don't know about you, but I find snacks are maybe the most challenging area for those of us who'd like to cut back on our consumption of UPFs. When you're out and about, in a rush and in need of an energy top-up or emotional boost, it's only natural to be tempted by an (often pricey) plastic-wrapped snack. Not all of these would be classed as UPFs, but most are, and the others may still have longer ingredients lists than we would like. Often the only less processed option is a piece of fruit, which let's be honest isn't always what we're craving!

Having a few go-to recipes for homemade snacks that are simple and can be made in a batch on the weekend (or whenever works with your schedule) is invaluable. For example, **making your own hummus** (page 200) is such an easy win: it's quick to make, budget friendly, super adaptable and I've never met anyone who doesn't want to scoop up a pile of hummus with some freshly made **flatbreads** (page 202).

I haven't tried to make homemade crisps here as nothing can recreate a packet of crunchy salty potato crisps, but making a sharing plate of hummus, fresh colourful veg, **Fetamole** (page 66), **Super Seedy Crackers** (page 215) with some olives and a favourite cheese is such a good alternative for an afternoon on the sofa or enjoying alongside drinks with friends.

If you're in a real pinch, there are a couple of snack recipes here that take no more than 5 minutes to make: the **Apple Nut Butter Dippers** (page 216), which are as good and addictive as they sound, and the walnut and Cheddar **Stuffed Dates** (page 208) are a great sweet and savoury fix.

If you are more often after a sweet treat for your snack attack, check out the Sweets chapter (pages 177–95) for a variety of transportable sweet options for on-the-go munching.

Snacks

Trio of fridge faves:
hummus, chilli sauce, pesto

Switching up your sauces is one very immediate way to reduce UPFs, as many shop-bought versions contain lots of extra ingredients we don't need.

———————

Pesto

Makes 1 big jar
Takes 10 minutes

3 large handfuls of fresh basil
1 handful of whole almonds or your fave nuts (preferably toasted if you have time)
2 garlic cloves, peeled
Juice of ½ big lemon
30g Parmesan, finely grated
6 tbsp extra virgin olive oil, plus extra for storing
Sea salt and black pepper

If you've got a strong blender or food processor, then use those delicious basil stems too as they're full of flavour and it means nothing goes to waste.

———————

Blitz all of the ingredients until smooth and season to taste with salt and pepper. Store in a covered jam jar with an extra drizzle of olive oil on top. This will keep in the fridge for up to 5 days, ready to be tossed through your fave pasta with a good splash of pasta water to loosen.

Hummus

Feeds 6–8
Takes 10 minutes

1 x 400g tin of chickpeas, or ½ x 660g jar of chickpeas, drained
3 tbsp tahini (stirred well in the jar first)
1–2 garlic cloves, to taste
Juice of 1 lemon
3 tbsp ice-cold water
Sea salt

Hummus means chickpeas but you might like to use the same recipe and try this with cannellini or butter beans.

———————

Put the chickpeas, tahini, garlic (starting with one clove), lemon juice and a good pinch of salt in a food processor or blender. Blitz until smooth, then, with the motor running, pour in the ice-cold water, 1 tablespoon at a time, until you reach a silky smooth consistency. Taste and adjust for seasoning, blitzing in more garlic if you like. Keep in a covered container in the fridge for up to 5 days.

Chilli sauce

Makes about 250ml
Takes 20 minutes

150g red chillies
1 tbsp tomato purée
3 garlic cloves, peeled
½ tsp sea salt, plus extra to taste
2 tbsp apple cider vinegar
6 tbsp water
1½ tbsp maple syrup

A homemade version of sriracha, the hot and tangy sauce from Si Racha, Thailand. This sauce can be kept in the fridge for a few weeks due to the vinegar's preservative qualities. I wouldn't use Scotch bonnet or bird's eye chillies here as they will be too fiery. It's also easy to halve or double, depending on your chilli addiction.

———————

Chop the stalks off the chillies, then blend all the ingredients together in a food processor. Transfer to a pan and simmer for 10 minutes, lid off, to thicken up. Let it cool, then taste for seasoning. You should taste hits of spice, garlic, tanginess and sweetness, so adjust accordingly.

Pour the sauce into a sterilised jar, cover and keep refrigerated for a few weeks.

Flatbreads with garlic herb butter

Makes 8
Takes 15 minutes

250g plain wholemeal, white
    or gluten-free flour, plus extra
    for dusting
1½ tsp baking powder
250g yoghurt
¼ tsp sea salt

FOR THE GARLIC HERB BUTTER
    (OPTIONAL)
1 garlic clove, finely chopped
3 tbsp butter, at room temperature
    or softened
Generous sprinkle of chopped
    fresh coriander, flat-leaf parsley
    or chives
Sea salt and black pepper

Many of the flatbreads and pittas you find at the shops are, sadly, often full of ingredients that make them UPFs. But the good news is that they're so easy to make at home in just 15 minutes. Serve with the Moroccan Lamb Meatballs on page 172, the Harissa Aubergine Dip on page 206 or the Whipped Feta Dip on page 210.

Mix all the flatbread ingredients together in a big bowl. Dust your work surface with flour and knead the dough for a minute. Add a little more flour if the dough is sticky, or a bit more yoghurt if it's dry. Roughly divide the dough in half, then half again and half again to make eight pieces of dough. Roll out each piece, adding a little flour to the work surface and rolling pin as needed. (A bottle of wine will also work for rolling out the dough.)

Heat a large, non-stick frying pan to a high heat, then cook one flatbread at a time for 1 minute or so on each side, flipping when you see bubbles and puffing. Keep them warm in a clean tea towel while you cook the rest.

If you want to make the butter, mix all the ingredients together in a small bowl with some salt and pepper. Add 1 teaspoon of butter onto each flatbread to melt. Alternatively, melt all the ingredients together in a pan while the flatbreads are cooking, then pour into a small bowl and then let everyone dip their flatbreads into it.

Sunshine tea

Makes 4+ mugs
Takes 15 minutes

1 lemon
1 clementine, satsuma or ½ orange
Thumb of fresh ginger
1 tsp ground turmeric
Small pinch of black pepper
Chilli flakes or cayenne pepper
1 cinnamon stick or ½ tsp
  ground cinnamon
1 litre just-boiled water
Honey, to taste

My go-to drink all year round. Enjoy hot or cold. Make a big batch of this citrus ginger tea to brighten up your kitchen. You can keep topping it up with hot water to get as much flavour as possible from the ingredients. The black pepper is said to activate the turmeric's health benefits and it adds a little kick. It's also a good one if you're feeling a little under the weather.

———————

Slice the lemon, clementine, satsuma or orange, and the ginger. Add the citrus, ginger, turmeric, black pepper, chilli flakes or cayenne and the cinnamon to a teapot or heatproof jug. Pour in the just-boiled water and stir. Leave to steep for 10 minutes, then strain into mugs with honey to taste. Keep topping up the pot or jug with water throughout the day.

Sunshine iced tea for sunny days: brew the tea as above. Allow to cool, then either strain over lots of ice and enjoy straight away or pour into ice-cube trays and freeze to later add to glasses of sparkling water.

Harissa aubergine dip

Feeds 6 as a dip
Takes 1 hour 15 minutes (only
15 minutes hands-on time)

2 aubergines
100g walnuts, roughly chopped
1½–2 tbsp rose harissa paste,
  to taste
Zest and juice of ½ lemon
Sea salt and black pepper

TO SERVE
200g yoghurt (plant-based
  if you prefer)
Drizzle of extra virgin olive oil
Flatbreads (see page 202
  for a homemade version)

It feels like those plastic pots of dips are everywhere. Sadly, they don't always hit the spot taste-wise, plus they often contain some of the ingredients we might want to steer clear of. Rose harissa paste is a jarred product I'd struggle to ever be without. Preparing aubergines can sometimes feel like a faff but essentially all we are doing here is mixing the cooled flesh of the aubergine with some incredible flavours. You could also do this with courgettes and sweet potatoes.

Preheat the oven to fan 220°C/gas mark 9.

Put the aubergines on a baking tray and roast for 45 minutes–1 hour until completely soft on the inside. (You could do this directly over the flame of a gas hob, which is faster, but I prefer the hands-off, faff-free alternative!)

Take a second baking tray and roast the walnuts for a few minutes or so until golden. Keep an eye on them so they don't burn in the high heat! Alternatively, toast them in a dry frying pan over a medium heat for a few minutes.

Once the aubergines have cooled slightly, remove and discard the skin. Put all the soft flesh in a sieve and leave for 10–15 minutes to drain off any excess water. In a medium bowl, mix the aubergine flesh, harissa (start with 1½ tablespoons), the lemon zest and juice and a pinch of salt and pepper. Taste for seasoning, adding a little more harissa and lemon juice if you like. Stir in most of the walnuts, holding some back for serving on top, and taste for seasoning.

Spoon the dip over the yoghurt and top with the rest of the walnuts and a drizzle of olive oil. Serve with flatbreads.

Snacks

Stuffed dates

Makes 12
Takes 5 minutes

12 Medjool dates
100g mature Cheddar, cut into
   small chunks or shards
12 toasted walnut halves or pecans

When you want something savoury AND something sweet too. This is a lovely combination of salty, sweet, crunchy and creamy. The perfect bite.

———————

Pit the dates and stuff each one with a chunk or shard of Cheddar and a nut. Enjoy straight away or keep in the fridge for up to 2 days.

Five-minute frying pan sticky spiced seeds and nuts

Feeds 4
Takes 5 minutes

40g unsalted butter
4 large handfuls of mixed seeds
   and/or roughly chopped nuts
3 tsp cumin seeds
3 tsp coriander seeds
2 tbsp maple syrup
Flaky sea salt, for sprinkling

A 5-minute, deeply moreish snack. Use any nuts or seeds you like. This serves four as a party (or sofa) snack but can easily be doubled or tripled if you're feeding a crowd. Lovely served with juicy olives. As well as being a fantastic snack, I scatter these on salads and soups too.

———————

Melt the butter in a frying pan and, once foaming, add the seeds and/or nuts and the spices. Fry over a medium heat for 3 minutes until lightly golden, stirring every now and then. Pour in the maple syrup and fry for another minute or so until it forms a sticky coating for the seeds and/or nuts. Spread out on a plate or tray lined with baking parchment and sprinkle over some flaky salt. Allow to cool, then serve, or store in an airtight container for up to 5 days.

Snacks

Whipped feta dip

Feeds 6–8
Takes 5 minutes

200g feta
3 tbsp thick yoghurt
Extra virgin olive oil
Sea salt and black pepper

OPTIONAL TOPPINGS
Za'atar
Harissa paste drizzle
Fresh herbs such as flat-leaf
  parsley, dill or coriander
Chilli flakes

A five-minute dip for all you feta cheese lovers out there.
Serve with the Super Seedy Crackers on page 215,
crunchy crudités like carrots, cucumber, radishes or
fennel or add to sandwiches or flatbreads (see page 202).

—————————

Blitz the feta and yoghurt together in a food processor until
smooth. Season to taste. Top with olive oil and your fave
spices and herbs.

Sweet potato wedges
with chimichurri

Feeds 4 as a side/snack
Takes 45 minutes

4 sweet potatoes (about 750g)
3 tbsp olive oil
¾ tsp flaky sea salt, plus extra
  for the chimichurri

FOR THE CHIMICHURRI
3 tbsp red wine vinegar
5 tbsp extra virgin olive oil
1 garlic clove, finely chopped
1 red chilli, finely chopped, or pinch
  of chilli flakes
1 large bunch of fresh parsley,
  finely chopped

This chimichurri recipe is based on the Argentinian green sauce – chimichurri verde – with lots of green herbs, tang from the vinegar and a generous dose of garlic and chilli for extra flavour. It's delicious on barbecue favourites and salads, on fried halloumi and grilled fish and is particularly good on steak. Use regular potato wedges if you like.

_____

Preheat the oven to fan 220°C/gas mark 9. Cut the sweet potatoes into chunky wedges, then toss with the olive oil and sea salt. Roast in your largest baking tray for 25–35 minutes (or use two medium baking trays as you want to space the potatoes out) until they are browned and tender.

To make the chimichurri, in a large bowl, whisk the vinegar, olive oil and garlic together. Stir in the chilli and parsley and season to taste.

Transfer the roasted sweet potato wedges to a plate and drizzle over the chimichurri, or you could serve the chimichurri on the side and dip the wedges in.

Super seedy crackers

Makes 1 large tray of crackers
Takes 40 minutes

100g chickpea (gram) flour
80ml olive oil
80ml water
3 tbsp mixed cumin, fennel, nigella
  and/or sesame seeds
50g pumpkin seeds
Flaky sea salt

Stored in an airtight container, these crackers can last for up to a week, although they never hang around for that long in our house. Have them on hand for snacking and dipping – they go especially well with the Whipped Feta Dip on page 210. Chickpea flour is also known as gram flour and is ideal for crackers and makes these naturally gluten-free too.

––––––––––––

Preheat the oven to 170°C fan/gas mark 5 and line a large baking sheet (about 40 x 25cm) with baking parchment or a silicone mat.

In a mixing bowl, whisk together the chickpea flour, olive oil, water and ½ teaspoon of flaky salt.

Pour the mixture onto the lined baking sheet and spread out to the edges (you want thin, crisp crackers). Sprinkle with the seeds and a little extra flaky salt. Bake on the middle shelf of the oven for 30 minutes until golden and crisp. Set aside to cool on the baking sheet, then roughly snap into crackers. Store in an airtight container for up to a week.

Apple nut butter dippers

Feeds 1
Takes 5 minutes

1 apple
2 tbsp your favourite nut butter (e.g.
  peanut, almond or cashew)
1 handful of granola (see page
  32 for homemade) or your fave
  seeds, such as pumpkin seeds,
  sunflower seeds or hemp seeds

So simple, and not really a recipe but a suggestion! You'll be making this daily before you know it. This is delicious with pear too. I particularly like pear with tahini and a drizzle of honey.

———————

Core the apple and cut into 6 wedges. Smear the wedges with nut butter and sprinkle over the granola or seeds.

Clementine chocolate dippers

Feeds 4
Takes 10 minutes, plus
setting time

100g dark chocolate, broken
  into pieces
4 clementines, peeled and pulled
  apart into segments
1 handful of finely chopped nuts
  (optional)
Flaky sea salt

Again, so simple this is hardly a recipe. Everyone knows and loves chocolate-dipped strawberries, but I think these are even better. Use clementines, satsumas or mandarins. I usually use pistachios if I make the nut option for a special occasion as I love the colour pop of pistachio green with the orange.

———————

Line a large baking tray with baking parchment.

Melt the chocolate in a bain-marie (a heatproof bowl set over a pan of barely simmering water). Half-dip the clementine segments into the chocolate and transfer to the lined baking tray. Sprinkle with the nuts, if using, then transfer to the fridge to set. Sprinkle with a little flaky salt before serving.

Cook's notes

I hope that if you are less confident in the kitchen, these tips and tricks will make your time in the kitchen count, and be more enjoyable too.

Everyone's **oven and hob** are different and you know your equipment best, so use the instructions given in this book as a guide and use visual cues and your instincts too.

Eggs are medium and room temperature.

Fruit and veg are medium sized, unless stated otherwise.

Fruit and veg are washed but not peeled, unless stated otherwise.

Citrus is unwaxed so that you can use the lovely zest and it's free flavour. Waste not, want not.

Garlic is peeled, unless stated otherwise.

Fresh ginger only needs to be peeled if it's not organic. It also freezes well.

Fresh herbs are whole (with stalks included, except those with tougher stalks like mint and rosemary), unless stated otherwise.

Source the best quality **animal products** (dairy, eggs, meat and fish) you can. I buy meat with the bone(s) in and skin on. For fish, I like to buy it with the skin on.

All **dairy products** are full-fat (whole) and all yoghurt is Greek or natural.

For **plant-based dairy alternatives**, check the labels and choose ones without added sugar, emulsifiers, stabilisers and other additives.

For **stock**, when I have the time, I like to make a big batch and freeze it in portions (see page 153). But for the occasions when homemade stock isn't an option, look for shop-bought versions without flavour enhancers, colourings and other ingredients you wouldn't have in your own kitchen. Ones in pouches generally have fewer additives than those in cubes, but as always read the label.

Dark chocolate is 60% cocoa solids or above. I like 70%.

Reheating – make sure your leftovers are heated right through. Leave a lid on the pan when reheating recipes like soups, porridge or stews to save time and not lose too much liquid. Simmer over a low heat for as long as it takes for the dish to get hot all the way through. Sometimes adding a little splash of water helps when reheating.

If you're **freezing leftovers or a batch-cook**, make sure the food has completely cooled before transferring to an airtight container (or bag/pouch for dry foods like flatbreads or banana bread). Label and date before freezing, as we always think we'll remember what's what but I never do! For best results, defrost in the fridge and don't refreeze a dish once it's been defrosted. Double check your fridge is set at its optimal temperature as this helps keep food fresher for longer and avoids food waste.

Meal prep tips

You might like to do some meal prepping on a Sunday evening or maybe it's something you have time for during a midweek work-from-home day. Either way, pick the tips that work best for you. I generally do 3 or 4 of the below and that takes me about 45 minutes hands-on time. I especially try to take advantage of having the oven on; I'll often roast some veggies to make use of the other shelf.

Assign one shelf or section of your fridge to 'ready to go' items – things that are grabbable, such as hummus (see page 200), salad dressing and Chocolate Peanut Butter Bars (see page 182). I like to do a shelf that's at eye level, so when I'm in a rush, I can immediately see what I can grab. This helps ensure things don't get pushed to the back and avoids food waste.

Freeze ripe bananas (peel and break them in half). These are brilliant for adding sweetness and creaminess to smoothies, porridge and baking (like my Banana Oat Breakfast Bake on page 26).

Double-batch a dip – e.g. hummus, fetamole, harissa aubergine (see pages 200, 66 and 206)– a dip always gets me eating more veg.

Cook up a batch of one grain or pulse (e.g. a container of quinoa or lentils or rice) to use to build a quick meal.

Wash salad leaves or chop crudités in advance so you have fresh veg ready to go for dips, quick salads or sides.

Make a simple sauce, such as the Red Lentil and Tomato Super Sauce on page 160, which can then be used as a base throughout the week, see page 20.

A pesto (see page 200) is a reliable standby to stir through pasta for a 15-minute dinner.

Bake something you like to snack on throughout the week (e.g. crackers on page 215 or granola on page 32).

Make a batch of salad dressing and refrigerate in an upcycled jam jar or bottle.

Pick a recipe for dinner that will give you leftovers for lunch the next day.

Roast a tray of root veg like squash, sweet potatoes or beetroot with your fave spice to add to lunches and as a side for dinner.

Roast or fry up some tinned or jarred chickpeas or beans – they give heartiness to salads or atop soups.

Bake a tray of baked potatoes (regular or sweet potatoes) to have with a salad and/or dip for quick working lunches (see the Green Goddess Salad on page 58).

Make croutons with leftover bread or pittas and keep in a jar or airtight container for a week to scatter over soups and salads.

Boil a six-pack of eggs and keep in the fridge with the shells on (less smelly and easier to transport). Add to salads, sandwiches and wraps.

Thank you to....

First, to Florence Blair for gracing your magic touch on every recipe and photo in this book. Your care and flair are unparalleled and I am the luckiest to get to work with you. Thank you for helping me bring *Real Healthy* to life and seeing me through IVF, pregnancy and early motherhood. You are brilliant and I really can't wait for your first cookbook.

Thank you Lizzie Mayson and Ollie Grove for not only your gorgeous photography but also your ideas for the rest of the book. It is a joy to work with you and pack up leftovers with you again. Thank you Tahira Harold for my shoot make up. Thank you Brigid Moss for reading an early copy. Thanks to both for the pep talks!

Emma Cantlay, I so appreciate your wonderful energy and artistic flourishes on set.

A ginormous thank you to friends and family – Mum, Lucy, Victoria Blair, Ruth Sanders, Shelley Martin-Light, Fiona Hemming and kids... all your dedicated testing made the recipes even better.

Thank you forever to Team Found Family, especially Alice Russell, KJ Arthur, Daisy Janes and Gee Burns. I have never felt so supported and I am grateful for your calm and capabilities.

My book family at Ebury Press, it is a delight to create our sixth cookbook together. Thank you to my incredible editor Celia Palazzo. Thank you for thinking of everything Vicky Orchard! Thank you for taking on the reins Emily Brickell and Liv Nightingall. What team work. For the beautiful, fun and cheerful designs, thank you Claire Rochford and Sophie Yamamoto. Thank you to the Ebury marketing maestros, Stephenie Reynolds and Mia Oakley.

Sarah Bennie PR – you are such a legend in the industry and it's an honour to work with you on all my books and run to get late night trains together up and down the country over the last 12 years.

Thank you enormously to nutritionist Rhiannon Lambert who has made *Real Healthy* complete with her fantastic foreword.

Thank you to all the people I admire who gave up precious time to read early proofs of this book and gave their votes of confidence and endorsements. With a special shout out to Professor Tim Spector and Tom Kerridge for their cover quotes.

Thank you to all the booksellers around the world, for stocking my cookbooks in your wonderful bookshops. Bookshops are my happy place.

The biggest cheers to my support team at home. To Henry Relph, Mum and Nelly, and to my baby daughter, Summer Eliza, who has just started weaning and makes me look forward to breakfast, lunch and dinner time more than ever!

Endnotes

*1 https://www.soilassociation.org/media/26802/upf_ffl_briefing_sa-3.pdf
*2 https://www.bbc.co.uk/food/articles/what_is_ultra-processed_food
*3 https://www.nutrition.org.uk/media/gcjhon0z/upf-position-statement_updated-post-sacn_130723.pdf
*4 https://foodfoundation.org.uk/sites/default/files/2023-12/PEAS%20PLEASE_PROGRESS%20REPORT_2023.pdf
*5 https://www.thelancet.com/journals/eclinm/article/PIIS2589-5370(23)00017-2/fulltext
*6 https://static1.squarespace.com/static/59f75004f09ca48694070f3b/t/6481134fdf3b065bf460fe05/1686180705852/FSN_
UPF+Report_Digital+for+web%2C+June+2023.pdf#page=43
*7 https://doi.org/10.1136/bmj-2023-077310

Dedicated to the memory of Emma Cannon

3

Ebury Press, an imprint of Ebury Publishing
One Embassy Gardens, 8 Viaduct Gardens
London. SW11 7BW

Ebury Press is part of the Penguin Random House group of companies whose addresses can be found at global.penguinrandomhouse.com

First published by Ebury Press in 2024
www.penguin.co.uk

A CIP catalogue record for this book is available from the British Library

ISBN 9781529940251

Editors: Celia Palazzo and Liv Nightingall
Project (and very patient) Editor: Vicky Orchard
Design: Claire Rochford
Artworking: maru studio G.K.
Photography: Lizzie Mayson, except author photo on page 7 by Ollie Grove
Food and Prop Stylist: Florence Blair
Food Stylist Assistant: Emma Cantlay

Colour origination by Altaimage Ltd, London

Printed and bound in Italy by LEGO spA

The authorised representative in the EEA is
Penguin Random House Ireland, Morrison Chambers,
32 Nassau Street, Dublin D02 YH68.

Penguin Random House is committed to a sustainable future for our business, our readers and our planet. This book is made from Forest Stewardship Council® certified paper.

MIX
Paper | Supporting
responsible forestry
FSC
www.fsc.org   FSC® C015829

'Joyful food at its finest and, just as importantly, healthy and supremely practical too – Melissa's recipes are my go-to for mid-week healthy meals that nourish body and soul.'
Dr Emily Leeming, PhD, RD, nutrition and microbiome scientist, registered dietitian and chef

'This book provides parents with nourishing recipes that their children will actually eat and enjoy; a feat in itself! I will be recommending it to everyone.'
Rhian Stephenson, nutritionist and naturopath

'The recipes are wholesome, colourful and full of plant points.'
Farzanah Nasser, nutritionist and certified functional medicine practitioner

'Valuable, passionate guidance on how we can unprocess our diets and better nurture our bodies.'
Anna Mathur, MBACP (Accred), psychotherapist

'Joyful rather than judgmental. A genuinely pleasurable way to eat better with zero compromises on flavour.'
Felicity Cloake, food writer

'To find a cookbook that makes it easier to return to real food cooking in a way that does not seem overwhelming is paramount. I look forward to incorporating these new recipe ideas into my repertoire for healthful food and an increased variety of plants for the health of my gut, brain and skin!'
Dr Tara Swart Bieber, neuroscientist, medical doctor, bestselling author of *The Source*, podcast host, and brand ambassador in beauty, health and wellbeing

'A deliciously informative and inspiring book, full of hacks and advice. I'm drawn to all of the vibrant veggie recipes.'
Mary McCartney, photographer, food writer and TV presenter

'Melissa's passion for combatting the prevalence of ultra-processed foods shines through in this book, and her message of promoting wholesome nutrition will resonate deeply with readers seeking a healthier lifestyle.'
Romy Gill MBE

'A book I'd recommend to anyone looking to ditch ultra-processed food and enjoy real healthy food.'
Adrienne Adhami, wellness coach and author